SO-BTP-426

Laramie Junior High
1355 N 22nd
Laramie, WY 82070

The Pampas, Andes, and Galápagos

MANAGING EDITORS

Amy Bauman
Barbara J. Behm

CONTENT EDITORS

Amanda Barrickman
James I. Clark
Patricia Lantier
Charles P. Milne, Jr.
Katherine C. Noonan
Christine Snyder
Gary Turbak
William M. Vogt
Denise A. Wenger
Harold L. Willis
John Wolf

ASSISTANT EDITORS

Ann Angel
Michelle Dambeck
Barbara Murray
Renee Prink
Andrea J. Schneider

INDEXER

James I. Clark

ART/PRODUCTION

Suzanne Beck, Art Director
Andrew Rupniewski, Production Manager
Eileen Rickey, Typesetter

Copyright © 1992 Steck-Vaughn Company

Copyright © 1989 Raintree Publishers Limited Partnership
for the English language edition.

Original text, photographs and illustrations copyright ©
1985 Edizioni Vinicio de Lorentiis/Debate-Itaca.

All rights reserved. No part of the material protected by
this copyright may be reproduced or utilized in any form
by any means, electronic or mechanical, including photo-
copying, recording, or by any information storage and
retrieval system, without permission in writing from the
copyright owner. Requests for permission to make copies
of any part of the work should be mailed to: Copyright
Permissions, Steck-Vaughn Company, P.O. Box 26015,
Austin, TX 78755. Printed in the United States of America.

Library of Congress Number: 88-18337

2   3   4   5   6   7   8   9   0   97   96   95   94   93   92

Library of Congress Cataloging-in-Publication Data

Beani, Laura, 1955-
  [Pampas, Ande e Galápagos. English]
  The Pampas, Andes, and Galápagos / Laura Beani,
Francesco Dessi, Massimo Pandolfi.

  — (World nature encyclopedia)
  Translation of: Pampas, Ande e Galápagos.
  Includes index.
  Summary: Describes the plant and animal life of the
Argentine pampas, the Andes Mountains, and the Galápagos
islands.
    1. Ecology—Argentina—Pampas—Juvenile literature.
2. Mountain ecology—Andes—Juvenile literature.
3. Island ecology—Galápagos Islands—Juvenile literature.
4. Biotic communities—Argentina—Pampas—Juvenile
literature. 5. Biotic communities—Andes—Juvenile
literature. 6. Biotic communities—Galápagos Islands—
Juvenile literature. [1. Ecology—Argentina—Pampas.
2. Ecology—Andes. 3. Ecology—Galápagos Islands.
4. Ecology—South America. 5. South America.]
I. Dessi, Francesco. II. Pandolfi, Massimo, 1944-.
III. Title. IV. Series: Natura nel mondo. English.
QH113.B4313   1988   574.5'2643'0982—dc19   88-18388
ISBN 0-8172-3325-3

WORLD NATURE ENCYCLOPEDIA

The Pampas, Andes, and Galápagos

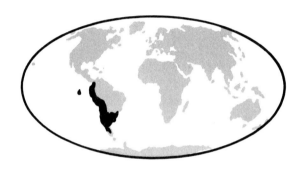

Laura Beani
Francesco Dessi
Massimo Pandolfi

Laramie Junior High
1355 N 22nd
Laramie, WY 82070

RAINTREE
STECK-VAUGHN
L I B R A R Y

Austin, Texas

CONTENTS

INTRODUCTION

The vast, largely grass-covered plains of the pampas are inhabited by the capybara (a tailless, four-foot-long rodent) and the viscacha (a burrowing rodent related to the chinchilla). There is a rich community of underground rodents and a wide variety of predators, including the gray fox and the jaguar. The rhea birds and other ground-dwelling birds run through the grass. Many different migratory birds are seen heading either north or south.

The pampas consist of dry and humid prairies stretching from the Atlantic Ocean to the Andes Mountains. The books of William Henry Hudson, a naturalist and writer from Argentina, offer a good description of the original pampas. These books create a picture of how the prairies appeared in earlier days. That was before they were crossed by highways and fragmented by barbed wire into pastures and cultivated fields.

Traveling through the Andes Mountains provides an opportunity to observe the vegetation zones of different plant communities. Each zone is made up of typical groups of associated plant species. These zones range from sterile

coastal deserts to luxuriant rain forests. So called "cloud" forests grow on certain mountain slopes that are permanently hidden by the clouds. There are also high, treeless plains in the mountains. These plains, called para amos, are cold and windy. They are also called punas, because of the puna grass that grows in these areas. The plants and animals of each zone show a series of adaptations to their particular habitats. These habitats may be located in areas characterized by dry climates, forests, or high elevations.

The Galápagos Islands, or the "Enchanted Isles," give the impression that time stopped there during the age of the reptiles. The landscape is very simple. Only a few species of plants and animals are found. Amazingly, few of the animals of the Galápagos appear to fear humans. This situation brings to mind the literary image of a "lost paradise." Animals live there that have evolved largely without the influence of human and natural predators. The Galápagos provide the setting for a unique expression of evolution in the world of nature. It could be lost forever if this area is not preserved.

THE PAMPAS
OF ARGENTINA

In the Quechua language of the ancient Incas, *pampas* refers to "plains." The pampas represent an extraordinarily uniform and compact environment. These plains extend for almost 301,000 square miles (780,000 square kilometers) between the Rio de la Plata to the north and the Rio Negro to the south.

The Boundless Plain

The terrain gradually rises in elevation from the shore of the Atlantic Ocean to the Andes Mountains. This rise is not noticeable until the Sierras Pampeanas of Cordoba and San Luis in central Argentina. These are a series of minor mountain chains parallel to the steep eastern slope of the Andean cordilleras (mountain chains). From the Portillo pass there is a complete view of the pampas, unless they are hidden by a layer of clouds. This mountain pass is like a door between Argentina and Chile. From here one can experience what the Uruguayan poet Juan Zorilla has described as "the solitude of the vast plain."

In effect, the geologic evolution of this area is characterized by a complex alternation of advancing and retreating seawater. About 400 million years ago, a large part of present Argentina was above water. It was a plain covered by glaciers, scattered marshes, and shallow bodies of seawater. Throughout the Mesozoic period (63 to 230 million years ago), a trench was developing where the Andes Mountains now stand. This trench extended in a north-south direction and was invaded by the sea. The rising of the Andes Mountains occurred between sixty and seventy million years ago. A huge depression was created on the eastern side of the Andes. The products of the erosion of these mountains built up in the depression. This accumulation formed the plain of the pampas. The wind brought fine sand from river deposits of the arid northern region to the area of the pampas. The plain was slowly covered by a mantle of "loess" (loamy deposits carried by the wind) that was tens of yards thick.

The pampas cover an enormous basin where sediments were deposited. The top layer of rock formed by these sediments is relatively thin. It consists of materials that were deposited by rivers and carried by the winds during the last 500,000 years.

The mountain range of the Sierras di Buenos Aires stands out on the horizon as a group of desolate and solitary rock masses. Sierra Tandilia is a crystalline rock formation

Preceding pages: Pictured are huts of the Uros Indians on a floating island in Lake Titicaca. With its size of 125 miles by 40 miles (203 km by 65 km), this lake is almost an interior sea. The Uros tribe withdrew to live on these floating islands. The islands were formed by thick reed beds that broke free from the shore due to the current or the wind. The Indians inhabiting them have developed what is called the "reed civilization."

Opposite page: While traveling across the pampas, the crested cariama is occasionally seen near ant or termite colonies. This bird is the last survivor of a line of large predatory ground birds that inhabited South America more than 25 million years ago. The habitat of the crested cariama is the dry pampas with scattered shrubs and bushes. It tends to avoid the forest and open grassland environments. Several aspects of its behavior indicate it is a social animal. It searches for food in groups or pairs.

Shown is a map of the precipitation of South America. From a climatic point of view, at least two zones can be distinguished in the pampas. To the east, there is a humid subtropical band with precipitation between 20 and 40 inches (500 and 1,000 mm). Up to 80 inches (2,000 mm) of rain may be received in the Uruguayan pampa. This eastern zone includes the basin of the Rio de la Plata and the province of Entre Rios (between the Paran and Uruguay rivers). To the west, there is a continental band. Here, there are cold winters, and the precipitation is lower, between 10 and 20 inches (250 and 500 mm). Precipitation in this zone decreases farther inland and farther south of the Rio Negro.

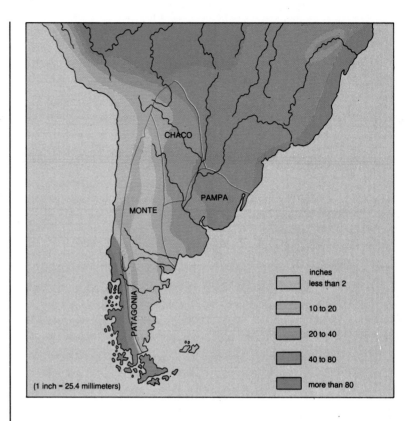

over 230 million years old. It is much older than the surrounding plain.

Further south lies the Sierra Ventana. This mountain was formed by highly deformed quartz rock of the Paleozoic period (230 to 600 million years ago) as well as by sedimentary rock.

At dawn, when the sun has not entirely risen above the horizon, the pampas have the appearance of a calm sea. Since the land of the pampas does not have a considerable slope, not all of the rivers reach the ocean. The rivers of the pampas are shallow and slow flowing. They filter through the ground or flow into marshes. In the winter after large rain showers, the rivers often change course. When this occurs, they flood clay-bottomed depressions. These large winter lakes of clear water give rise to expanses of brilliant green grasses.

The permanent rivers include the Rio Salado and the Rio Colorado to the south and the large Rio Paraná to the north. The Rio Paraná is a majestic, muddy river. Along with the clear Rio Uruguay, it forms the "estuary" of La Plata. (An estuary is formed at the lower end of a river where the river

The Rio Colorado owes its name to the red color of its water. Along with the Rio Negro, it represents the southern boundary of the pampas. The Rio Colorado begins in the Andes Mountains, in the province of Mendoza and then crosses an arid region. After a very difficult course of over 800 miles (1,300 km), it opens into a large delta. A delta is a triangular deposit of sand and soil found at the mouths of some rivers. Its banks are lined with willow trees and reed beds. In the summer, in December, when the snow in the mountains melts, the river forms temporary ponds and marshes.

current meets the ocean tide.) At Montevideo, the estuary is so wide that the other bank cannot be seen. It is a vast expanse of red water, the same color as the land through which the Paraná flows.

The Humid and the Arid Pampas

The pampas are a combination of green prairies and arid steppes (grass-covered plains). This alternation complicates the apparent uniformity of the landscape. The nearby Atlantic Ocean and the humid ocean winds create a subtropical band along the coast. This zone is characterized by hot summers, mild winters and abundant rainfall. The climate farther inland is continental. This means the winters are cold and the air becomes drier and drier toward the interior. The humid pampa to the east is separated from the arid pampa by an imaginary north-south line. This line runs from the city of Bahia Blanca to the lagoon of Mar Chiquita, northwest of Buenos Aires.

There are two winds that produce variations in the climate. One is the "pampero," a cold, dry wind that blows from the southwest. The other is the "zonda," which is a warm, humid wind from the north. These winds are perio-

This map indicates various vegetational environments of South America. Originally, the pampas were treeless prairies composed of various species of grasses (for example, *Stipa, Aristida,* and *Andropogon*). The pampas lie between the region of the Gran Chaco to the north and the arid steppe of Patagonia, south of the Rio Negro. To the west, there is a drought-resistant type of vegetation. This vegetation grows in several areas of the Gran Chaco. The area is also characterized by a discontinuous, or broken, grass cover with spiny shrubs up to 10 feet (3 m) high. This is the so-called monte zone that is damaged by fires and repeated cutting.

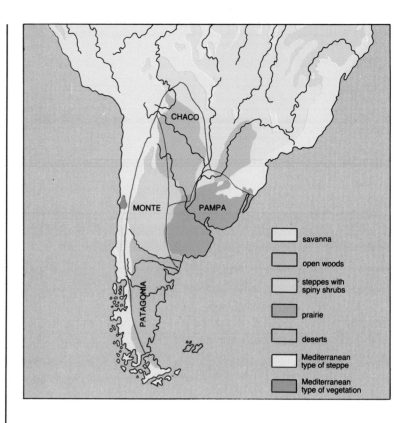

dic, meaning they happen at regular intervals. They occur because of the presence of Antarctic and tropical air masses, respectively.

On the plain, the summer begins in November. The grasses are dead by this time and have taken on a yellowish brown color. The prairie becomes a dusty dirt road. William Hudson, a naturalist who was born on the pampas and lived there many years, wrote, "It was then, when the watercourses were gradually drying up and the thirsty days coming to flocks and herds, that the mocking illusion of the mirage was constantly about us."

A mirage is an optical effect created by the bending of light rays by a layer of heated air. Hudson has described the typical mirage of water. It occurs when the air near the ground surface warms and becomes visible and dense. In the distance, the air takes on the appearance of shiny lakes. A group of trees on the horizon, a wind mill, a silo, or a low farmhouse appear as islands or hills. The cattle and horses that graze nearby seem to be standing in water up to their knees. After several days of this sultry weather caused by the winds from the north, the pampero begins to blow from

A rare Geoffroy's cat is seen among cardoon plants. The coat, which is finely spotted with black, is orange-yellow in the subspecies of the animal in northern Argentina. In the southern subspecies, which is found as far south as Patagonia, the coat is a silver-gray. This cat is more often found in the monte zones than in the forests and prairies. In the monte, the vegetation is scrubby with shrubs and other drought-resistant plants. The Geoffroy's cat prefers the scrub along the western edge of the Gran Chaco and in the eastern part of the Andes chain. It usually inhabits areas that are far from cultivated fields. However, it is occasionally seen around the more isolated farms.

the south. Dark clouds appear in the sky and drop a brief, heavy rainfall. This produces pools of water and many days of nice weather.

The summer is over in February, and the rainy season begins in the eastern climatic band near the Atlantic. Meanwhile, toward the Andes Mountains, the precipitation remains below 20 inches (500 millimeters). The arid region is called "the province of the Pampa." However, botanists label as pampas only the environment of the provinces of Buenos Aires and Santa Fe. These areas form a unique and immense prairie that was originally treeless.

In the arid pampa, the soil is dry and porous (full of holes), and the wind creates temporary dunes. Clumps of brownish yellow grasses cover the dry, sandy soil for several months of the year. Only a few low trees and thick, spiny shrubs can withstand the dry conditions of this region. This environment gradually changes to one with mountain-type vegetation.

The humid pampa is green from April to November. This vast expanse of green grasses, however, is not at all similar to an English meadow. There are bare patches that have been overgrazed, as well as dark marshy areas and

In the monotony of the plain, a group of trees, primarily poplars and eucalyptuses, grows around farm buildings. Rows of trees are generally used as windbreaks. They signal the presence of a farmhouse hidden among the green. "Estacias" are typical farms of 12 to 23 sq. miles (30 to 60 sq. km). A typical smaller farm of 1 sq. mile (2.5 sq. km) is called a "chacra agricola." Until the mid-1800s, the plains of the pampas remained uncultivated. Indian tribes of the Araucano group lived there. Today, these tribes have almost completely disappeared.

dense blue-green cardoon bushes. Cardoons are large perennials cultivated for their edible root and leaves.

Hudson wrote, "Pausing among the cardoons in the growing season, one could almost hear them growing, since the leaves sprung away from their contracted position with a snapping sound. It was a little like the cracking of the spiny seed cover of the broom plant that one hears in England, except much louder."

The landscape is very uneven. The variety of environments is made more complex by the changes introduced by human activities. Starting with the intense European colonization of the mid-1800s, the prairie has gradually been replaced by cultivated corn. This is especially true in the area near Rosario in central Argentina. Fields of barley and other grains are found in the southern zones. There the summers are dry, and the winters are rainy. The native prairie with its tough, sturdy vegetation was progressively replaced by pastures of tender plants. This new pasture consisted of a mixture of grasses that alternated with legumes. (Legumes make up a large family of herbs that

includes beans, peas, and clovers.) The biggest change, however, was the arrival of trees. The European settlers introduced poplar, eucalyptus oak, ash, as well as peach and other fruit trees. While crossing the pampas in 1832, Darwin was amazed by the almost complete lack of trees.

It is not surprising to learn that in the valley of the Rio Negro an isolated and ancient tree was respected by the Indians. It was honored as an altar to the god Walleechu, considered to be the protector of humans and horses. At one time, bleached bones of sacrificed horses were scattered around the trees. Various offerings were hung from the tree branches, such as cigars, bread, meat, pieces of cloth, and even a single thread from a poncho.

The trees became part of the landscape of the pampas because, as Hudson described, "The first colonists who made their homes in this vast, vacant space called the pampas came from a land where the people are accustomed to sitting in the shade of trees, where corn and wine and oil are supposed to be necessities . . ." Gradually, the environment began to take on a completely different appearance.

ANIMALS OF THE PAMPAS

The vast grasslands of the pampas are not inhabited by large herbivores or herds of hoofed animals. The pampas never were large like the North American prairies of a century ago, or like the African savannas of today. However, some fossils of large animals were found at Punta Ala. A few skeletons were buried among the clay deposits of the pampas. Darwin did examine some fossils of giant animals when he visited the pampas. At one time, many such species of animals thrived in this region.

Giant sloths, armadillos, large, hoofed herbivores, and flesh-eating marsupials (animals whose young develop in a pouch) no longer inhabit these areas. Sometime before the Isthmus of Panama connected South and North America, these species inhabited South America. For many millions of years the animals of South America evolved in isolation. This was a critical period for the evolution of the higher vertebrates. When the isthmus slowly emerged from the sea, between three and five million years ago, a land bridge was created. This bridge enabled a new redistribution of animal species. Afterward, there was a brief period during which animals migrated in both directions. Gradually, a large part of the primitive South American animals became extinct.

Herbivores of the Pampas

As in other animal groups, the hoofed animals of the pampas include both native and nonnative species. The nonnative varieties either spread to the area naturally or were imported by humans. The wild horse, which originally came from North America, mysteriously became extinct throughout all of the Americas.

Camel-like animals spread throughout the grasslands of South America between thirteen and twenty-five million years ago. The native genus of the llama originated in these regions.

The bovine animals (buffalo, cattle, sheep, and goats) of the North American grasslands did not spread into South America. The forests of the isthmus were a barrier to them. In recent centuries, enormous herds of domestic cattle grazed on the pampas.

Ricardo Guirades' novel *Don Segundo Sombra* is dedicated to the legend of the "gaucho," a cowboy of the pampas. The book describes the pampas as a landscape of cattle and cowboys in movement. Today, the cattle no longer roam over the plain. Their pastures are almost all fenced. Wild herbivores are found only in parks.

Opposite page: The armadillos are among the few survivors of the large group of animals that at one time included sloths and anteaters. This peludo armadillo is widespread throughout Argentina. The armor of this species is covered by hair. Another hairy armadillo is the pichi, which weighs from 2 to 4.5 pounds (1 to 2 kg). It prefers to inhabit sand dunes. In case of danger, the pichi quickly buries itself or it securely wedges the toothed edges of its shell into the ground. The peludo armadillo is brown and larger than the pichi. It weighs between 5.5 and 8 pounds (2.5 and 3.5 kg). It hunts snakes, cutting them in two with the sharp edges of its shell. The three-banded armadillo has a heavy shell and is hairless. It defends itself by rolling up into a ball. The seven-banded armadillo has large ears and a thin, hairless shell. The shell of this species is used in making stringed musical instruments.

A gaucho guides a herd of pasturing cattle. In the pampas, cattle ranching did not become an economically important industry until the mid-1800s. The first colonists of the area allowed their herds to roam in a semiwild state. In time, this method changed to a more organized system. Gauchos, or cattle herders on horseback, live on the prairies of southern Brazil, Uruguay, and Argentina. They are often of mixed Indian blood.

Deer spread into South America from North America and successfully adapted to the new environments. The species are small or average in size and have simple antlers. The extremely shy pudu is a tiny deer that barely reaches 15 inches (40 centimeters) at the shoulder. The gray Andean deer is now very rare. It is found only in certain reserves in the mountains of Peru, Chile, and Patagonia. The marsh deer is on the verge of extinction due to extensive hunting. The pampas deer is well represented only in the Mato Grosso Park in Paraguay and in several parks of the Uruguayan pampas. The Rio Negro represents the biogeographic (referring to geographic distribution) boundary of this species.

The Rodent Population

Only a limited number of large, wild, hoofed animals lives on the pampas. This is in contrast to the large numbers of rodents. They are not as readily visible, however. As in the desert, the absence of trees or a thick cover of vegetation encourages the development of an active underground community. Since the surface of the ground is patrolled by predators, the maze of tunnels and dens underground assures the inhabitants of the prairie a secure refuge for raising their young.

The many varieties of Central and South American rodents evolved partially during South America's long period of isolation. What the animals look like and the environments in which they live in South America are both similar to those of the Old World.

Until the end of the last century, the viscacha, a burrowing rodent, was extremely numerous across the plain. Today however it is found most often in parks. The black-and-white stripes on the snout of the viscacha give it the appearance of having a moustache. Outside the den, this able burrower scurries away from danger with its tail erect.

The viscacha lives in groups of twenty to thirty animals. Their colonies are composed of a network of interconnected family dens. The dens have spacious, circular rooms and several entrances. Mounds of dirt are usually piled around the entrances. The viscachas more than tolerate the presence of other animals. They actually share their dens with rodents, lizards, burrowing owls and snakes. Foxes also take advantage of the viscacha dens. They peacefully live together with the viscachas until spring. At this time, the young viscachas venture outside and become easy prey for foxes.

Approaching a viscacha colony at sundown, old males can be seen sitting motionless in front of the den with the smaller, more cautious females behind them. A pair of burrowing owls are often found roosting on a mound of dirt nearby. The miner ovenbird uses the mounds of dirt in which to dig its nest. These mounds are rare in the pampas. The abandoned nests of the miner ovenbird are often reused by the small swallows of the *Atticora* genus. These birds can occasionally be seen at the entrances of dens.

As soon as an intruder approaches a viscacha community, the viscacha on guard alerts the rest of the group. Every viscacha immediately disappears into the den. It seems that these animals make different alarm sounds

The prairie is inhabited by a large community of rodents. Some of these share the dens of the viscachas *(bottom right)*. *From top to bottom and from left to right:* The mara, which looks like a cross between a small antelope and a hare, has in many ways occupied the ecological niche of the hare. The agouti shares the viscacha dens in the pampas. East of the Uruguay River, where the viscacha is not found, the agouti digs its own nest in the ground. The burrowing owl uses the tunnels of prairie dogs. The southern cavy is shown feeding on a bush. A nutria with its young is illustrated near a stream. The tucu-tuco is a social rodent that digs extensive tunnels near the surface like a mole. The tucu-tuco is extremely slow and awkward when walking over the ground. In fact, it only moves its hind legs sideways, as if it were swimming. Two viscachas (a female and a male, respectively) are pictured. An ovenbird, of a dirt brown color, surveys the ground.

according to the type of predator that approaches. This behavior has already been established in the case of ground squirrels. A typical practice of the gauchos consisted of bringing guests from the city to a colony of viscachas on the plain at night when it was dark and silent. Suddenly a gaucho would shoot once with a gun. Hudson wrote, "...and after two or three seconds, the report would be followed by an extraordinary hullabaloo, a wild outcry of hundreds and thousands of voices, from all over the plain from miles round, voices that seemed to come from hundreds of different species of animals. So varied they were, from the deepest booming sounds to the high shrieks and squeals of shrill-voiced birds. Our visitors used to be filled with astonishment."

Today, the viscachas live in marginal areas or in reserves. The farmers hunt these animals because of their habit of razing all the plants surrounding their colonies. The strong incisor teeth of the viscachas enable them to chew cardoons, corn, and other cereal grains. The stems are cut to pieces and piled at the entrance of the den, together with any other objects that they can carry.

Perhaps it is only a legend, but a story is told of a man who lost his watch while horseback riding at night. He found it by looking around a viscacha colony along the road. The viscacha, like the thieving magpie in Europe, has earned the reputation of being a habitual collector.

It is unknown why these animals collect and pile such an incredible variety of objects in front of their dens. Many theories have been proposed. They include blocking the entrance, decorating the den, and distinguishing one den from another. Perhaps the most convincing theory is the one proposed by Hudson. Hudson believed that the piles of objects are a further protection for the dens against dust and heavy rainfalls. He also suggested that the cutting of all the tall pampas grasses is done in order to be able to see predators from afar.

Other small animals slowly modify the landscape of the pampas. The tuco-tuco rodents burrow near the ground surface, like moles, leaving mounds of dirt on top of the ground. Their name derives from the typical sounds made by these nocturnal animals. The sounds resemble hammering noises. Hudson wrote that the noise sounded "as if a

The capybara is an excellent swimmer. In case of danger, it readily jumps into the water. This animal spends most of the afternoon grazing in the grass along rivers. In the morning, the capybara basks in the sun and later cools itself by entering the water. It is widespread from Venezuela all the way to the Río de la Plata. The vast, dusty plains of Venezuela are transformed into marshes in May. In these plains, the domestic capybara is partially replacing the traditional domestic animals. Raising capybaras as a food source is profitable in areas of seasonal pastures. Thirty-two capybaras in an area that is 0.6 mile (1 km) wide produce 3 tons (2,700 kg) of body mass per year.

a group of gnomes was working there underground, hammering on anvils, at first loud and then soft and light."

Hudson listened attentively to all of the natural sounds of the pampas. These included even the softest sounds, such as those made by the southern cavies. This small rodent makes a muted, subtle sound, "almost like the murmur of a brook." Like all cavies, it prefers arid environments with bushes for hiding and playing. This animal is very active and social.

Life Along the River: Capybaras and Jaguars

The most commonly seen animal along the large rivers of the pampas is the capybara. It is perhaps the largest rodent in the world. Several specimens weigh over 110 pounds (50 kilograms) each and measure over 3 feet (1 m) from the nose to the end of the tail. They are highly visible, especially in the early morning and at dusk, when grazing

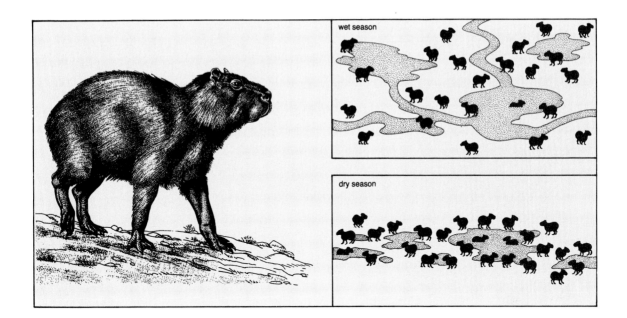

wet season

dry season

The capybara has a large, stout body, and its toes (four on the front feet and three on the back feet) are partially webbed. This is an adaptation to aquatic life. Recent studies on the behavior of this large rodent have shown that during the wet season, the population is distributed in small groups near temporary pools and streams *(top right)*. During the dry season, most of the population is concentrated along the banks of permanent rivers and small lakes *(bottom right)*.

among the tall grasses along the riverbanks. They prefer freshwater rivers to saltwater rivers. A Swedish botanist classified the capybaras as "water hogs." This was because of their stout shape and light skin, which is covered by sparse, brown hair.

Capybaras are social animals that live in groups of several families. The dominant males occupy the center of the herd near the females. The other animals remain on the margins and are more exposed to danger. Capybaras rarely fight. A rival male will step backward when the dominant male takes a step in its direction.

Occasionally, it seems that the capybaras nod to each other. Actually, they mark the boundaries of their territories by spreading a scent produced from a black, berrylike gland on the snout. The young are protected at the center of the group.

Capybaras do not burrow dens. Water is their refuge. When danger is sensed, the animals warn each other by a grunting or a puffing sound. They immediately jump into the river together.

The traditional enemy of the river rodents in the Argentine and Uruguayan pampas is the Paraná jaguar. This excellent swimmer presently survives in the El Palmar park and in a few other reserves of Argentina and southern Brazil. At one time, the jaguar populated the reed thickets along lakes and the wooded banks of large rivers. Its coat of black

pampas cat

South American cat (kodkod)

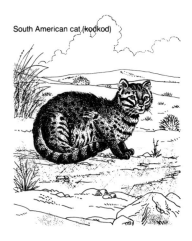

Many species of small, native cats have become quite rare, even within nature reserves. They include the pampas cat and the South American cat, both of the genus *Felix*. The pampas cat inhabits open prairies and the tall steppes of the Andes. Its silver-gray coat is long and soft. When excited, the hair on its back stands up. Unlike the other South American cats, the pampas cat has pointed ears (like domestic cats) without tufts of hair. The South American cat, or kodkod, is yellowish brown and is more widespread on the Chilean side of the Andes. It inhabits forests and scrubs. Geoffroy's cat inhabits the monte environment of the pampas. The Andean cat is found up to an elevation of 16,400 feet (5,000 m) in the western part of the pampas. It has an ash gray coat with orange-yellow spots. In Argentina, it is often confused with the pampas cat.

spots allows it to blend in well with the surrounding vegetation.

In the stories of the gauchos, the jaguar is always portrayed as a legendary character. The gauchos have long been fascinated by the hunting skills of this animal. This is perhaps due to the jaguar's ability to kill only the animal it wishes to eat out of an entire herd. The puma, on the other hand, kills many more animals than it actually consumes. The jaguar does not flee from the scent of humans. Instead, it follows the trails used by people through areas of dense vegetation.

The numerous rodent populations are preyed upon by an entire series of wildcats from the same genus. Many of them are native species. The varieties of species that can belong to one genus (as in the case of felines, canines and rodents) results from spreading out into a territory during the evolution of the individual species. When a new type of animal colonizes an area without strong competition, it quickly takes over in the various habitats. Once they have occupied these habitats, the new animals evolve their own peculiar characteristics. In South America, there were many unoccupied habitats as well as habitats occupied by more primitive and less-efficient predators. The ancient marsupial carnivores are an example of primitive predators. As mentioned earlier, these animals were not able to compete with the newly arrived wildcat. The wildcat, therefore, began to occupy all the various habitats.

The puma belongs to the same genus as the jaguar. It is unique among the various wildcats of the pampas, since it is also found in North America. It is not a native species in South America. The puma feeds on bison, deer, and young bears, as well as rheas, guanacos, viscachas, and other small mammals. Many of these predators have been greatly reduced in number and are now mostly found within the boundaries of parks.

The natural environment of the pampas is also found in protected parks as well as in marginal areas. Unfortunately, the size of these areas is quite restricted. Most of the land of the pampas in Argentina and Uruguay has been changed into cultivated fields and grazing land.

The gray fox is still fairly widespread in the humid pampa. It is a great hunter of viscachas and cavies as well as birds. The gray fox also eats plants, which give it a more flexible diet. The most specialized of the South American prairie canines is the maned wolf. Because of its long legs,

Shown are several typical stances of the maned wolf. This highly endangered species is found on the prairies and in the marshes of southeastern Brazil, Paraguay, and Bolivia. It also inhabits the humid pampa of Uruguay and Argentina *(see map). From top to bottom and from left to right:* Walking gait, with the snout leaning toward the ground and both legs of one side moving at the same time; menacing posture, with the snout, neck, and back in the same line; female and young of ten weeks, whose legs are not yet lengthened; playful pose; while eating, the maned wolf keeps the front legs bent; finally, the maned wolf becomes familiar with its environment by sniffing while moving about.

Following pages: A rhea is pictured with its young. In five months, the young will reach the size of an adult.

this animal resembles a fox on stilts. Its legs are adapted for running in the tall grasses of the Brazilian savannas, in the humid pampa of northern Argentina, through marshes and in the thickets along rivers. Overgrazing by domestic animals has resulted in a lower height of the grass cover. This has reduced the size of the ideal habitat of the maned wolf. This animal does not hunt in packs since its prey is rather small. It will eat rodents, birds, lizards, insects, and fruit. The maned wolf is probably the least social of all canines.

The crab-eating fox is an omnivore, meaning that it eats both plant and animal substances. Its diet includes crustaceans, frogs, and small rodents. In the Argentine pampas, it inhabits the same habitats as the gray fox. However, in the open prairie, it prefers the dense vegetation along the rivers. Farther north, the crab-eating fox lives in the forest.

The bush dog is also adapted to humid environments, but its diet is primarily carnivorous. It is an excellent swimmer. Despite its small size, it hunts capybaras, pakas, and rheas. Unlike the maned wolf, the bush dog has short, strong legs that are adapted to moving through dense vegetation. It lives and hunts in groups that form extended families. The bush dog has a short tail and ears and is dark in color. These traits are also found in the forest dog.

Large Birds of the Prairie

Groups of rhea birds are often seen among the gray thistles and the herds of sheep and horses. Their gray-and-white plumage allows them to hide in the vegetation. The rheas are cautious birds. They are especially wary when approached by someone on horseback. Traditionally, these birds were hunted by the gauchos with the use of bolas. The rheas are known for their cleverness and their running speed. While running, they lean their heads forward and raise one wing like a small sail. This wing is used to suddenly change direction.

During the mating season, the male rhea makes a deep hissing sound. Darwin wrote, "When I first heard it . . . I thought it was made by some wild beast, for it is a sound that one cannot tell whence it comes, or from how far distant." The males fight each other in order to dominate a group of females. During their fights, the males move around and around while twisting their necks, biting, and kicking. The defeated males lose the opportunity to approach the females. The winner builds a nest in a hole in the ground and lines it with dry grass. The male mates with five or six females, which lay their eggs in the nest. Up to sixty eggs accumulate in the nest. The eggs are brooded by the male for a period of forty days. The male is also responsible for raising the young. The young are able to leave the nest soon after they are born. In the meantime, the group of females, which are generally sisters, may move away to mate with three or four other males. They will lay eggs in each of the males' nests. All of this may occur during the same long mating season.

The advantage of this reproductive system is the multiple production of nests and eggs. This occurs because the females need not build nests, brood eggs, or raise young. This increases the chances of the reproductive success of the species. The male spends much energy and time in incubating the eggs and caring for the young.

The tinamou birds have a similar reproductive system. The males dominate a group of females. Several of the females lay eggs in the same nest. The male tinamous are responsible for brooding these eggs. The tinamous belong to an order of South American ground-dwelling birds. They include about seventy species. All of the species are characterized by earth-colored brown plumage. Their dimensions range from the size of a quail to that of a pheasant.

The males defend a small territory in which they mate

black-necked screamer

snail kite

American jacana

black-headed duck

and nest. The females move about in small groups between the nests of different males. Since the nests are built on the ground, they are easily preyed upon. The young develop quickly and the males care for them without the help of the females. The most common species in the pampas are the tataupa tinamou, the spotted nothura, the crested tinamou, and the greater tinamou. The tataupa tinamou is also called the "house bird" because of its habit of approaching human dwellings.

Other birds of the pampas spend much of their time on the ground. They take flight only when necessary. They nest among the grasses or on the lowest branches of bushes and trees. One of these birds is the crested cariama. It moves through the grass on its long legs in search of insects, snails, and small snakes. It is the only surviving member of a primitive group of gigantic predatory birds that inhabited these grasslands more than 25 million years ago.

The black-necked screamer is a bird that has difficulty becoming airborne. Of this bird Hudson wrote, "For here was a bird as big or bigger than a goose, as heavy almost as I was myself, who, when he wished to fly, rose off the ground with tremendous labor. As he got higher and higher he flew more and more easily, until he rose so high that he looked no bigger than a lark or pipit. At that height he would continue floating round and round in vast circles for hours, pouring out those jubilant cries at intervals which sounded to us so far below like clarion notes in the sky."

Perhaps the unusual flights of the black-necked screamer are due to the extraordinary combination of its light bones, air sacs, and pneumatic (air-filled) skin cells. This bird builds its nest on the ground. It is usually placed among marsh grasses or it may float in the marsh water. The male and female live together and share in brooding the eggs.

Colorful Birds

The monotonous green color of the pampas is enlivened by the smaller birds. A group of trees, almost like an island in the pampas, is ideal habitat for many small species of birds. A small space can hold many surprises for the naturalist. When spring begins in August, the flowering pear trees are filled with green, gray-breasted parakeets. With their sharp beaks, they can strip a tree of leaves in a few minutes. These birds live in colonies. They build a tangle of heavy nests out of twigs on the highest tree branches. Each nest hosts up to a dozen pairs of parakeets.

25602

Above: The pampas flicker originated on the prairies of southern Brazil and Argentina. It feeds mostly on termites. The yellow-shafted flicker and the rock flicker belong to the same genus. The yellow-shafted flicker is found in North America and Central America. The rock flicker lives along the slopes of the Andes Mountains up to an elevation of 15,420 feet (4,700 m).

Opposite page: Shown are several of the typical birds that gather in the spring and summer around the lagoons of the pampas. Reeds and sedges grow around these small, shallow lakes. *From top to bottom:* the black-necked screamer, which is similar to a large goose; the snail kite, a slate-colored bird that resembles the buzzard in size and flight and feeds only on aquatic snails; the American jacana, a strange reddish black, rail-like bird with very long toes, wing spurs, and yellow wattles; the black-headed duck, perhaps the only example of an aquatic bird that lays its eggs in the nests of other birds, such as ducks, limpkins, and gulls.

LJHS-1995   574.5/WOR   15.00

Flocks of yellow and green goldfinches can be seen roosting on a tree and singing in unison. Occasionally, they might fly off together in a colorful cloud and land in the tall grass of the pampas.

In the summer, the brown-headed crowbirds land on the rows of mulberry and poplar trees. They search for nests where they can lay their eggs. They belong to the family Icteridae that also includes American blackbirds, orioles, and grackles. The birds of this family are widespread throughout the American grasslands. Like the cuckoo, they occupy nests built by other birds. The female brown-headed crowbird is gray, while the male is a dark violet color. When they form a flock, they look like a shiny black carpet on the grass. Occasionally, many of them can be seen perching on the backs of horses or cattle.

The fire-crowned tyrant also does this. It is called "the little horseman" because of its habit of riding on the backs of livestock all day long. The fire-crowned tyrant has a showy red crest of feathers that can be raised straight up. It shows its red crest during courtship, food conflicts, and

Laramie Junior High
1355 N 22nd
Laramie, WY 82070

while defending its young. It builds a nest of grass and leaves wherever possible. Sometimes nests are built under the eaves of houses or in tree cavities. The fire-crowned tyrant becomes quite aggressive, taking over the nest of a larger bird to build one of its own.

Most of the ovenbirds are distinguished by their different nest-building styles. The nests range from dens dug in the dirt to globs of moss suspended from tree branches. Some nests are shaped like the traditional ovens used for baking bread. This is particularly evident in the nests of the rufous ovenbird. Starting in the fall, this rust-colored bird accumulates mud on whatever solid base it can find. The collecting of mud is continued throughout the winter. By spring, almost every streetlight has one of these peculiar

A pair of rufous ovenbirds occupies a nest. This species is one of the most easily approached birds of the pampas because they are very social. The nest is sometimes oval and sometimes globular with a diameter of 8 to 12 inches (20 to 30 cm). The walls are made of mud and plant fibers, and are about 4/5 inch (2 cm) thick. Naturalists have observed that as a whole, the nest resembles a traditional bread oven. This observation is what led to the bird's name. The nest lasts for more than one year, and it often is used by swifts the following season.

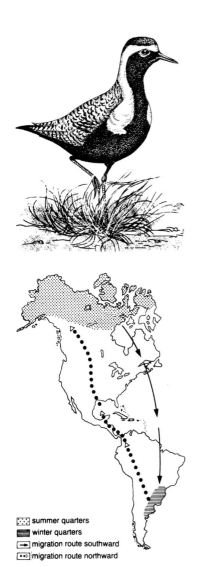

The American golden plover begins its long migration on the coasts of Labrador and Nova Scotia at the end of the mating season. It reaches the coast of South America, and after a brief stop, it flies farther south along the Amazon basin. It arrives in the Argentine pampas in September. In January, it flies to the tundra of northern North America where it will nest. On the return trip, the plover flies over the Amazon River, the Antilles, and the great plains of North America. It thus completes an oval migration route across the Western Hemisphere. At the time of the migration southward, the adults take off before the young are able to follow. The young leave later and find the way to Argentina on their own.

:::: summer quarters
▓▓ winter quarters
→ migration route southward
•••▷ migration route northward

"igloos" sitting at the top. These nests have a side entrance, a front room, and a narrow passageway leading to the main room, which is lined with soft grass.

In August, migrating birds arrive from far northern areas. The vermilion flycatcher is probably the showiest of the migrating birds. It is bright red with black wings and tail. The colors of its plumage sharply contrast with the leaves of the trees it inhabits. The swifts also return to this area in August. When the acacia trees are in bloom, the emerald hummingbirds arrive. These birds beat their wings so fast that they seem magically suspended in the air.

In September, the more humid pampas fill with American golden plovers. In March, the plovers leave to migrate back to the north. They fly very high in the sky, completing a spectacular round-trip migration of about 14,900 miles (24,000 kilometers). In May, they are replaced by birds migrating from the deep south to flee the cold Antarctic winter. These birds include the Falkland plover and the winter plover.

The Patagonian parrot also arrives during this period. This bird makes a partial migration toward the Rio de la Plata. Until the beginning of this century, flocks of them could be seen flying over Buenos Aires. Shrill shrieks announce their arrival long before they appear in the sky. The Patagonian parrots have long, pointed wings and a dark-green plumage. Their feathers are speckled with yellow, blue, and red.

Thus, the windy grasslands of the pampas, which may not seem attractive to birds, host many different migrating bird species. In March, April, and May, there is a long succession of bird flocks in the sky. Some are leaving for the north, while others are arriving from the south.

The teru-teru is another plover commonly found in this area. Its name derives from the piercing cry it makes. It is present year-round and nests in the humid eastern pampas. Another unusual call is made by the great kiskadee, a tyrant flycatcher. Like birds of prey, this bird flies in circles for a long time before dropping on its prey. It hunts mice, lizards, and small snakes. At dusk, it roosts on bushes along the edges of roads. It constantly repeats its song. The steady, repetitive song of the great kiskadees is added to the calls of the viscachas and the small rodents. It is also joined by the shrill cries of the black-necked screamers and the hoarse cries of the teru-terus. The sounds of the finches and the parrots complete this "music of the pampas."

THE ANDEAN CORDILLERA

The chain or cordillera of the Andes Mountains cuts across half of the Western Hemisphere in a north-south direction. It extends from the warm coasts of the Caribbean Sea to Tierra del Fuego at the southern tip of South America. The cordillera of the Andes crosses seven countries. Latitudes range from 10 degrees north to 55 degrees south at Cape Horn. At the equator, the snow limit in the Andes is at an elevation of between 13,120 and 16,400 feet (4,000 to 5,000 m). At Tierra del Fuego, the snow limit is a little higher than 3,280 feet (1,000 m). The chains and peaks that form the Andes Mountains extend uninterrupted for 4,350 miles (7,000 km).

Darwin remarked how the Andes chain formed a perfect barrier, a large solid wall surmounted by a tower of rock here and there. He noted that groups of peaks and volcano cones are separated by long distances.

The Longest Mountain Chain in the World

It would be a mistake to think of the Andes chain as a single, linear structure. Actually, the Andes are divided into numerous cordilleras, which either run parallel or merge together. East of Venezuela lies the Cordillera de Merida. To the south, in Colombia, the main body of the chain divides into three parallel ridges. They are the Cordillera Oriental (eastern chain), the Cordillera Central (central chain), and the Cordillera Occidental (western chain). These chains come together to form one mass at the border with Ecuador.

Thus, Colombia does not have a warm and humid climate with tropical vegetation. Instead, it is a mosaic of environments where extremely different plant and animal species overlap.

The central chain is enclosed within the narrow valleys of the Rio Magdalena and the Rio Cauca. These rivers are actually two huge cracks or rifts in the earth's crust. They are similar to the Rift Valley in eastern Africa. They include tropical lowlands within the heart of the Andes chain. In this area are several of the most beautiful Andean volcanoes. Examples are the Nevado del Ruiz at 18,374 feet (5,600 m) in elevation, the Nevado del Huila, the Tolima, and the Santa Isabel.

Farther south in Ecuador, the Andes chain branches into two cordilleras that are almost parallel. The western branch includes the volcano Pichinca, which towers 15,765 feet (4,805 m) above Quito, the capital of Ecuador. Iliniza at 17,242 feet (5,255 m), and the great Chimborazo at 20,703

Opposite page: Shown is the picturesque valley of the Urubamba River. This valley begins in the Andes, near the Raja pass. The river flows north and northwest along a north-south valley before uniting with the Apurímac to form the Ucayali River in the Cordillera Occidental. This valley is representative of the marginal or exterior zones of the Andes, which are characterized by deep gorges. The central zones of the Andes, instead, are rich with plateaus and have few gorges.

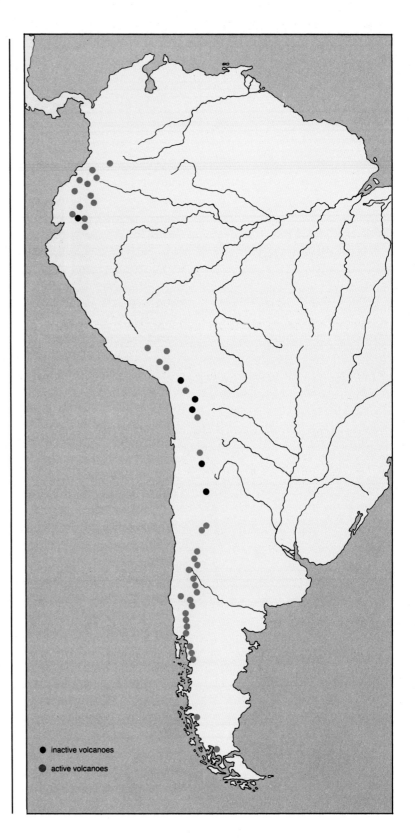

At 4,350 miles (7,000 km) long, the Andean Cordillera is the longest mountain chain in the world. It is a young mountain system, as evidenced by the numerous volcanoes. Several of these are still active. The mountains that form the cordillera represent an unpassable barrier for the masses of humid air coming both from the Pacific and the Atlantic coasts. Consequently, the zones that are immediately "leeward" (in the direction toward which the wind blows) of the mountains have desert characteristics.

inactive volcanoes

active volcanoes

The map shows the formations of volcanic rocks present in the Andes. Volcanic activity has occurred since these mountains were formed, 50 to 100 million years ago. The western part of the Andes has mostly volcanic rock and granites. The central part has more secondary rocks of limestones and sandstones. The most ancient rocks are found in the eastern part.

feet (6,310 m), which is the highest peak in Ecuador, are also found in this branch. The eastern branch includes Cayambe at 18,980 feet (5,785 m), Sangay at 17,465 feet (5,323 m), and the perfect cone of Cotopaxi, with an elevation of almost 19,685 feet (6,000 m). At the end of the last century, the explorer Edward Whymper appropriately described Cotopaxi as "the perfect volcano." Many of these volcanoes, such as Sangay and Cotopaxi, are still active. This activity causes severe earthquakes over a large part of the Andes.

In Peru, Bolivia, and northern Chile, a vast area of rolling, high-elevation plains extends between the western and eastern cordilleras. This is the Peruvian plateau, which measures 124 miles (200 km) across at its widest point. Between the elevations of 12,140 and 13,780 feet (3,700 and 4,200 m), it is covered by an arid and low grassland called the "puna." Only in Tibet, can a similar vast plateau at such a high elevation be found. This area is dotted by permanent lakes that are fed by torrents of the high Andes. One of these is Lake Titicaca. With a length of 124 miles (200 km) and a width of 37 miles (60 km), this lake is almost an inland sea. Other lakes are Junin in central Peru, and Saracocha between Puno and Arequipa.

North of Lima, the western chain is cut lengthwise by the valley of the Rio Santo. This separates the Cordillera Negra from the Cordillera Blanca. The Cordillera Negra reaches an elevation of almost 14,800 feet (4,500 m), and its peaks do not have snow year-round. The peaks of the Cordillera Blanca are very high and covered with snow. They include Huascaran at 22,206 feet (6,768 m), the volcano El Misti at 19,168 feet (5,842 m), and Sajama at 21,389 feet (6,519 m). Glaciers form on their slopes for relatively brief periods due to the steepness. There also are very clear glacial lakes surrounded by stones deposited by earlier glaciers.

East of the Peruvian plateau, the Andes chain divides into two cordilleras. The Cordillera Real is where Anchouma at 21,490 feet (6,550 m) towers above Lake Titicaca. The impressive volcano Illimani, which reaches 22,967 feet (7,000 m), is found in the second cordillera, the Cordillera Vilcapampa. As they descend in elevation, the Andes slope toward the great basin of the Amazon River. The rainfall and humidity are high on this eastern side of the mountains. Therefore, the vegetation there is particularly luxuriant. This is in contrast with the vegetation on the Pacific side of the mountains.

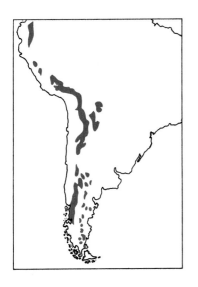

Pictured is a mountain peak at an elevation of 18,373 feet (5,600 m) in the Cordillera Real, Bolivia. Cup-shaped formations of the glaciers are evident in the photograph. These formations are totally absent in the Alps of Europe.

In the southern part of Chile and Argentina along the lower slopes of the Andes, subantarctic forests of southern beech, Chilean pine, and podocarpus trees grow. These forests thrive in zones where the temperature has a yearly range between 9° and 41°F (-13° and 5°C). These zones are characterized by heavy snowfall and an annual precipitation that reaches 78 inches (2,000 mm). At elevations between 3,280 and 6,560 feet (1,000 to 2,000 m), the beech trees are much shorter and are more like shrubs. They form dense, impenetrable thickets.

Opposite page, from top to bottom: Illustrated are the branch, fruit, and a fruit section of the chinchona tree. This tree is noted for its medicinal properties in treating malaria. Below that is the branch, section of flower, and fruit of the guava tree. From this tree, the Indians extracted a delicious gelatin.

In the southernmost section, the Andes chain tends to become less dramatic. However, it still represents an imposing barrier between the pampas and the Pacific Ocean. The highest peak in the Americas is located in Argentina near the border with Chile. Aconcagua, at an elevation of 22,842 feet (6,962 m), tops all of the nearby peaks: Ojos del Salado at 22,580 feet (6,882 m), Bonete at 22,520 feet (6,864 m,) and, farther south, Tupungato at 22,310 feet (6,800 m).

By following the ancient, steep routes of the Indians, which zigzag across the Piuquenes and Portillo chains, some of Darwin's world of 1835 can be experienced. At that time, Lyell's revolutionary book *The Principles of Geology,* had just been published. It stated that the outline of land surfaces was determined by the effects of atmospheric agents and water over long periods of time. For Darwin, who traveled with a copy of Lyell's book, the torrents of the Andes were a visible and spectacular proof of the forces involved.

Darwin was not as fascinated with the life of the Andes as he was with the geology and the fossils of these mountains. Perhaps this was due to his greater experience as a geologist, rather than a botanist (a scientist who studies plants) or a zoologist (a scientist who studies animals), at the time of his trip. Furthermore, there were not many possibilities for observing animals because of their relative scarcity.

These mountains are rich, however, with desert and subdesert environments. Under such conditions, the backbone of the terrain is more evident. The bare slopes, the steep rock walls, and the overlaying, colored layers of sedimentary rocks are striking.

The Botanist's Paradise

The Andes extend over the earth for more than 4,350 miles (7,000 km). Describing the Andean vegetation can be as difficult as making one's way through a complicated maze. The wide range of elevations in the Andes, from sea level to 22,967 feet (7,000 m), must also be considered. It is practically impossible to briefly describe the hundreds of different plant environments that grow along these mountain slopes. Considering the great number of different climates at different latitudes and elevations in the Andes, it is easy to picture several different plant environments. These range from very dry, rocky deserts to lush, tropical rain forests. Also included are the cold, southern forests of Chile pine and Patagonian beech trees. Finally, there are warm,

chinchona tree

guava tree

equatorial savannas at low elevations and cold grasslands at high elevations. This complex vegetational picture can be considered a botanist's paradise. Botanists have renamed the entire Cordillera area in order to study the plants that grow in the different zones. This has involved a great deal of difficulty and discomfort.

Until the nineteenth century, the Western world considered South America a new and relatively unexplored continent. Its uniqueness, due largely to its geographic isolation, is reflected in the great variety of its plant and animal species.

Studies of the vegetation by western countries were further delayed by the political situation that existed in South America. The Spaniards were extremely protective of their rich overseas possessions. They directly controlled all access to South America.

In 1770, King Charles III organized a large botanical expedition under the direction of the naturalist Hippolito Ruiz. In 1794, Ruiz published one of the first accurate books on South American plants, *Flora Peruvianae et Chilensis* (Plants of Peru and Chile).

In 1799, the German baron Alexander von Humboldt was authorized to carry out a study of the Andes. This was the first time that a non-Spanish scientific expedition was permitted to venture forth into these regions without bureaucratic obstacles. Von Humboldt was a scholar of zoology, botany, and geology. He was one of the first naturalists to explore the northern Andes. He began in Cartagena, Colombia, where the Rio Magdalena empties into the Caribbean Sea. He ventured as far as Lima on the Peruvian coast. The Spanish botanist José Celestino Mutis also participated in the expedition. In those years, Mutis was collecting information for his splendidly-illustrated botanical book, *Flora de Nuevo Reino de Granada*. It referred to what was, at that time, the country of Colombia. The book had 5,190 illustrations and 171 sketches of plants. Curiously, this book was neglected by the museum of natural science in Madrid. It was finally published in 1952, over two hundred years after the death of the author.

FROM COASTAL SLOPES TO HIGH GRASSLANDS

The vegetation of the Andes is affected by the mountains. The tall, parallel chains constitute a natural barrier that obstructs the circulation of large air masses. This barrier creates particular climatic conditions that largely determine the types of plant communities that grow on the slopes. It is not possible to understand the distribution of plants and animals in the Andes without first understanding its peculiar climates.

The Coastal Deserts

Along the Pacific side of the Andes, 1,864 miles (3,000 km) of coast is arid and consists of desert. This strip extends from a latitude of six degrees south to twenty-eight degrees south. In contrast, the eastern side of the Andes slopes, which looks out over the vast Amazon basin, is a luxurious tropical rain forest. The aridity (dryness) of the western side is due to a combination of various factors. One of these factors is the coastal barrier of the Andes. The Andes obstruct the movement of large masses of humid air from the east. These masses originate in the Amazon Basin. On the Pacific side, the coastal waters, which are affected by the Humboldt Antarctic Current, are much colder than the continental air mass. Consequently, the marine air mass becomes heated when it contacts the coast but is unable to condense into clouds. It moves up the steep slopes of the Andes while remaining dry. It cools at a high elevation, and it is only at this point that it forms extensive fog, the famous "garuas." Thus, the coastal deserts were created.

The Peruvian-Chilean desert has a unique appearance. In several zones, it is barren and desolate. Millions of smooth pebbles stretch as far as the eye can see. Other zones are sandy with regular and crescent-shaped dunes shaped by the wind. These dunes strongly resemble the dunes of the Sahara Desert in Africa. Signs of life are not totally absent, however. Scattered screwbean shrubs and a peculiar vegetation of ground bromeliads (*Tillandsia* genus) grow in the most favorable areas. The bromeliads are in the Spanish moss family, and they form dense cushions of vegetation. Here and there, the large arms of candelabrum-shaped cacti (of the *Cereus* genus) as well as prickly pear cacti (*Opuntia* genus) appear.

The grayish tufts of the *Tillandsia* bromeliads have a diameter of about 12 inches (30 cm). They are seen all along the coastal deserts. The ancestors of these plants grew on trees and other plants for support. Such rootless plants are

Opposite page: This photograph is of the sand and pebble desert near Casma, at the foot of the Cordillera Negra in Peru. It shows the barrenness of the dry territories of the Pacific side of the Andes.

41

called "epiphytes." The bromeliads that grow in these deserts have adapted to growing on the ground. Like their ancestors, the desert bromeliads do not have roots for absorbing water or anchoring themselves. They are supported on the ground in an unstable manner. Therefore, they are able to roam about. They take in water through their leaves. Almost all of this water comes from absorbing the night dew and the fog.

Without roots or trees to grow on, the *Tillandsia* bromeliads are carried by the wind in one of the most arid deserts of the world. The light fog provides their only nutrition. These plants are said to be the only true "fog plants."

The South American desert expanses of pebbles and sand are undoubtedly the most barren in the world. Although the animals are scarce, they are not altogether absent. The burrowing owl can be seen as it perches

The arid coastal headland of the Paracas Peninsula in Peru is seen. Today, it is an important national park for the archaeological findings of pre-Columbian civilization.

Opposite page: The ground bromeliads of the genus *Tillandsia* are perhaps among the most common colonizing plants of the sandy deserts. They survive the desert conditions by taking in the little water necessary for their growth through absorbing plates on the leaves.

motionless atop a rock. This bird preys on scorpions, insects, and small mammals such as sand rats. The sand rats burrow in the small, sandy hills. They are one of the most important links in the food chain of the desert.

The Loma

On the Andes slopes, a dense permanent layer of fog is found at an elevation of a few hundred yards. Inland from the coast, the desert loses its harshness. The sparse tufts of *Tillandsia* plants are soon replaced by an unusual blackish vegetation. It consists of patches of a brown algae belonging to the genus *Nostoc*. This algae has a gelatinous (jellylike) consistency and covers rocks and sand with a thin film.

The vegetation here consists of extremely primitive plants that do not produce seeds. Their presence suggests that something has changed in the desert environment, although precipitation remains low. This zone is characterized by the so-called fog vegetation. An example of this type of vegetation is found north of Lima near Pachacamáe. This band of primitive vegetation is followed by sparse tufts of herbaceous or nonwoody, green plants. Above an elevation of 656 feet (200 m), the herbaceous plants gradually become thicker. This transition finally ends with a dense vegetation of these green plants and trees. This area is called the "loma."

Climatically, the zone can be considered a desert. It receives less than 1 inch (25 mm) of annual rainfall. And yet, a true oasis of plants is encountered here. These plants are supported solely by the water droplets present in the fog.

Between elevations of 1,969 and 2,625 feet (600 to 800 m), the fog cover persists uninterrupted for months. In this band, the plants are extremely luxuriant. Fields of bushes and several types of trees grow in this area. They include mesquite and the bird-of-paradise tree. The latter has branches that are densely covered by mosses and lichens. There are also small plants such as *Peperomia cristallina*. At this point, the native trees of the Andes have almost completely disappeared from the loma zone. For centuries, they represented the only wood resource of the local people. Unfortunately, the eucalyptus and beefwood trees have replaced the original tree species. Today, only a small section of the original forest remains near Atiquipa.

Until recently, it was not known how the plants of the loma survived without rain. The fog alone did not seem

43

Shown is a schematic representation of fog distribution along the Andean slopes. For a large part of the year, a layer of clouds and fog covers the slopes facing the Pacific Ocean. This causes the air temperature to increase with elevation. At the lower elevations, the vegetation is scarce or lacking entirely. It gradually becomes thicker as the elevation increases. The plants growing here derive their water supply strictly from the condensation of moisture from the fog.

sufficient to maintain the vegetation, which did not have any particular physical adaptations. The plants do, in fact, survive with only the fog as a source of moisture.

Every day, a weak southern or southeastern wind from the coastal area, carries a constant supply of fog to the mountain. The air masses that rise along the slopes cool as the elevation increases. Therefore, the water vapor is transformed into small droplets of fog. The water droplets produced by this condensation are deposited primarily on the obstacles encountered along the way. The droplets are driven by the whirlwinds that blow around them. The taller or larger an object, the greater the condensation. When condensation occurs, the water drips to the ground.

The humid cycle continues as long as the fog lasts. At the beginning of the summer months, the fog gradually thins out until it disappears. This is the start of the dry season in the lomas. The dry season in the lomas coincides with the rainy season in the Northern Hemisphere.

After several months, the fog rises once again along the slopes. With the reappearance of water, a new growing season begins.

Above an elevation of 2,950 to 3,600 feet (900 to 1,100 m), the fog breaks up and gradually disappears. The dark

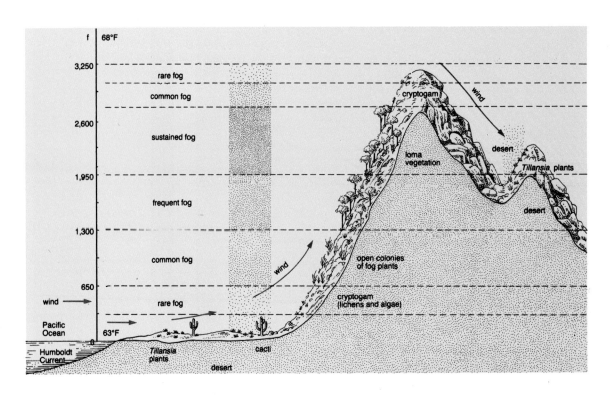

and mysterious world of the fog is replaced by an environment of desert vegetation. It includes *Tillandsia* plants and cylindrical cacti of the *Cereus* genus. Some species of this genus reach heights of 13 to 16 feet (4 to 5 m). The next tree vegetation is found starting at an elevation of 9,840 feet (3,000 m) where the cloud forest begins.

The loma does not regularly support a particular group of animals. Since it is a narrow oasis of plants between two bands of desert, however, it does serve as an important environment for the refuge and migration of numerous species. They arrive in this lush, green zone from the north as soon as the winter, dry season starts in those areas. Even the pre-Incan civilization made use of this strange climatic situation.

During the growing season, numerous hummingbirds fly to this area. An example is the shiny, bluish purple *Rhodopis vesper*. The beautiful white-winged dove builds its nest on low trees. In this area, the vermilion flycatcher is also found. This bird is the size of a sparrow and inhabits environments of arid woods.

Pictured is a small lake at high elevation within the Manu National Park of Peru. It is almost completely hidden by the cover of fog and clouds typical of the Andean slopes.

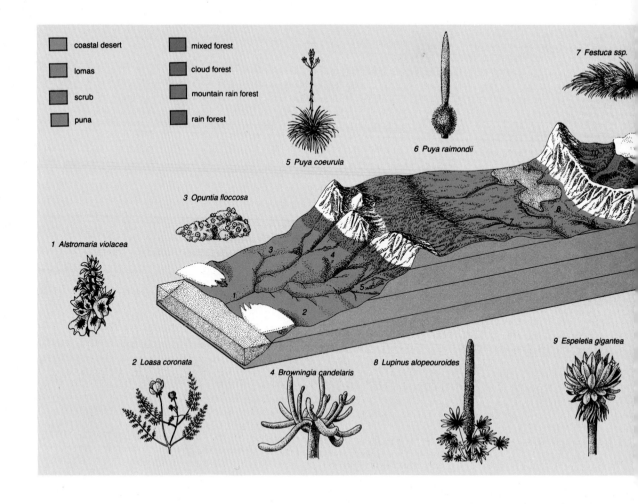

coastal desert

lomas

scrub

puna

mixed forest

cloud forest

mountain rain forest

rain forest

7 *Festuca ssp.*

6 *Puya raimondii*

5 *Puya coeurula*

3 *Opuntia floccosa*

1 *Alstromaria violacea*

2 *Loasa coronata*

4 *Browningia candelaris*

8 *Lupinus alopeouroides*

9 *Espeletia gigantea*

The Andes Cordillera represents a barrier between two regions that have opposite climates and vegetation. The western slopes facing the Pacific are among the most arid areas in the world. The eastern slopes are characterized by a humid climate that allows the growth of lush forests. The Andes Cordillera itself, due to its length and elevation, is a succession of vastly different climatic environments. Each environment is characterized by a particular vegetation.

The lomas experience vertical migrations. These are migrations of birds that come down from the high mountains during the winter season when the higher elevations have become arid and severe. Among these birds are the semillero, a finch with a brilliant, light blue back, and the small, crested, Peruvian sparrow.

Several rodents, such as the degu, are common and characteristic inhabitants of the lomas. They dig extensive underground dens where they store food. The degus resemble rats. Unlike the common rat, however, the degus can climb trees. It is not unusual to see them in the trees toward dusk.

The Tropical Forest

At the equator, farther inland from the influence of the cold Humboldt ocean current, the western slopes of the

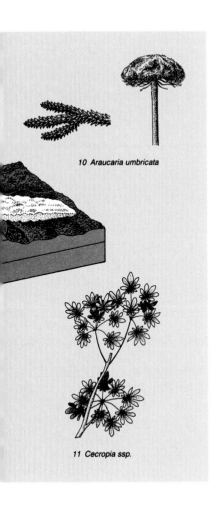

10 Araucaria umbricata

11 Cecropia ssp.

Andes are covered by a dense, tropical forest. This forest is found between 8,200 and 9,187 feet (2,500 and 2,800 m) of elevation. Originally, the tall trees of this forest formed an unbroken cover.

The tropical rain forest that extends from the Pacific coast to the Andes of northeastern Colombia is one of the zones with the highest precipitation in the world. Near Buenaventura, in western Colombia, over 355 inches (9,000 mm) of annual rainfall have been recorded. The average annual rainfall of the zone is 197 inches (5,000 mm). This regular and abundant rainfall produces an extremely lush forest. The forest is characterized by very tall trees covered with woody vines, mosses, and orchids.

This environment has various aspects. Along the slopes at an elevation of about 5,906 feet (1,800 m), the tropical rain forest is replaced by a subtropical (referring to regions bordering the tropics) or temperate, forest that is found up to an elevation of 7,218 to 8,200 feet (2,200 to 2,500 m). The trees in this forest reach heights of 131 feet (40 m).

The Cloud Forest

Perhaps no other forest in the world offers the visitor the same sensation of strangeness and mystery as the cloud forest of the Andes. This landscape is almost always immersed in the shadows of vast clouds. Tall, dark trees are covered by many different species of bromeliads, whose leaves are rose-shaped clusters. The plants in this forest take on interesting shapes as the dark sky is crossed by continuously moving fog.

There is high humidity in this vegetation zone, although the precipitation is not very heavy. This zone offers ideal conditions for the growth of numerous epiphytic plants. These plants derive moisture from rain and usually live on another plant. These include bromeliads, begonias, orchids and ferns. They almost completely cover the trees, especially if the trees are isolated. One species of bromeliad, *Tillandsia usneoides*, forms long beards that hang from tree branches. It has a root system that supports the plant on the tree or else anchors it among the ridges of the bark. Its hanging tufts can extend over all of the branches, giving the tree a unique, decorated appearance. This plant species also has a peculiar method of multiplying. New plants grow from pieces of an existing plant. Birds help this plant multiply by breaking off pieces of it to build their nests.

The biological adaptations of the epiphytes are quite

The howler monkey is one of the noisiest animals known. Its call starts with a gurgling noise and then changes into a hollow, rumbling sound. This sound can be heard from a considerable distance. The sound originates in the upper part of the windpipe. The muscles of the stomach and breast powerfully force the air through the upper opening of the bony voice box. The voice box of the howler monkey *(top)* is twenty-five times larger than that of a woolly monkey *(bottom)* with the same body size.

Opposite page: Shown is a tree of the cloud forest decorated by streamers of epiphytic plants. These plants grow on other plants for support but not for food. These plants belong to the genus *Tillandsia.*

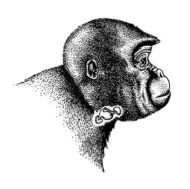

interesting. These plants live with almost no soil from which to absorb water and nutrients. They must, therefore, form their own soil reserve and absorb water in other ways. This means they can only live in environments with abundant rainfall or high humidity. Many epiphytes have long aerial roots. All epiphytic plants have elaborate adaptations that limit water loss. They include thick, waxy coatings on the leaf surfaces and fleshy leaves.

Plants that lack underground roots must also evolve special adaptations to absorb mineral salts from the soil. Several species of epiphytes, such as the large bird's-nest fern, collect nutrient debris from around their roots and leaves. The staghorn fern, which is a common houseplant, has a large basal (arising from the stem) leaf that folds around the stalk of the plant. This leaf has a rather short life. However, after it has dried, it remains firmly attached to the plant. The dead leaf then collects nutrient matter such as humus. Humus, which is decayed plant material, supplies nutrients to the plant.

The plant formation of the cloud forest begins in the northernmost sector of the Andes—in the Sierra Nevada de Santa Maria in Colombia. Climbing the trails of these mountains to an elevation of about 9,187 feet (2,800 m), one encounters a long layer of low clouds that permanently divides the mountain horizontally. After entering this world of low, whirling clouds, visibility becomes limited to only a few yards. The soil is soft and moist, and the tall trees drip dew.

In its original state where human activities have not modified it, the cloud forest is filled with animals. It is inhabited by numerous monkeys, such as the capuchin monkey, the howler monkey, the squirrel monkey and the small marmoset. Marmosets have long, prehensile (adapted for seizing or holding objects) tails. These animals are often found in large groups.

The Paramo

The tropical forest and the cloud forest are left behind as one continues to climb the slopes of the Andes. The true high-elevation environments then begin. These high-altitude forests and meadows are called "alpine environments" by botanists. They are perhaps the most characteristic environments of the cordillera. The Andean alpine meadows can be divided into two types. One is the "paramo" of Venezuela, Colombia, and Ecuador. The other

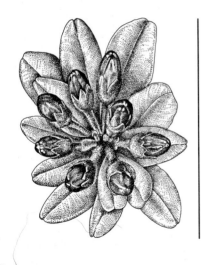

is the "puna" of the more arid, colder regions of Peru, Bolivia, and Chile.

The paramo is a cool and humid meadow extending above an elevation of 9,840 to 10,500 feet (3,000 to 3,200 m). Here the altitude causes considerable temperature variations. The daytime temperature of 68° to 77° Fahrenheit (20° to 25° Celsius) often drops below 32°F (0°C) at night. The meadow is crossed by clouds and fog that bathe everything in moisture. A fine, penetrating drizzle is often transformed into snow. The sun only makes short appearances.

In this high-elevation, tropical environment, the grass cover is extremely green. There are no trees, but, like the high-elevation savannas of the large African mountains,

A remarkable stretch of thousands and thousands of plants of the genus *Espeletia* characterize the paramo near Bogota, Colombia.

Opposite page: Numerous plants of the paramo display circular clusters of flowers or leaves. This arrangement decreases the effect of the wind and protects the plant from sharp drops in temperature. The drawing shows the rosettes of a plant of the genus *Vaccinium.*

there are several herbaceous plants that over time have developed treelike shapes.

Examples of treelike forms include the plants of the *Espeletia* genus. These plants are several yards (meters) tall. They are very similar to the giant senecios that grow on the slopes of Mount Kilimanjaro and Mount Rwenzory in Africa. This similarity is a curious example of parallel evolution that occurred in areas having the same environmental condition but far away from each other. These conditions are high humidity, intense solar radiation, and a high daily variation in temperature. Thousands of miles separate these environments, yet the *Espeletia* plants and the giant senecios are remarkably similar. Instead of having a circular cluster of basal leaves at the ground level (as in normal composite plants), the *Espeletia* plants and giant senecios basal leaf clusters are much higher off the ground. When the old leaves die, new leaves are formed above the dead ones. This creates a central stalk. This stalk is surrounded by dry leaves that are folded toward the ground. The tip of the plant keeps growing upward, producing clusters of long, lance-shaped leaves.

Pico Bolivar is 16,428 feet (5,007 m) high and overlooks the small, charming village of Merida. This peak is part of the Cordillera de Merida, which represents the northeasternmost branch of the Andes. Pico Bolivar is located within the national park of the Sierra Nevada, which offers a good example of the high Venezuelan paramos. Various species of *Espeletia* and low heath shrubs with delicate pink or white flowers, grow here. Spiraea shrubs, gentians, small erigeron plants, and herbaceous senecios are also present.

Some of the most interesting plant species of these meadows are the lupines. Lupines have an erect flower spike with large, blue flowers. These flowers stand out among the low expanse of the paramo. One lupine species, *Lupinus alopecuroides*, produces a dense, conical, silky flower cluster that is more than 3 feet (1 m) high. This flower cluster is similar to that of the treelike bromeliad of the genus *Puya*. It also resembles the giant lobelias of Africa. This is another example of parallel evolution.

The large, robust flower spikes that rise up out of the sea of grass are easily seen by the insects and hummingbirds. The silky appearance of these plants results from the dense, silvery hair that covers their leaves. The hair serves to reduce water loss and shields their tissues from the ultraviolet rays of the sun.

51

Shown is the yellow expanse of grasses of the Peruvian puna near the Conococha Pass. All of the grass species are called "ichu" by the local people although they belong to different genera.

The Puna

In Peru, Bolivia, and Chile, the high-elevation meadows of the Andes are composed of a poorer, semidesert type of vegetation. This vegetation is conditioned by scarce precipitation. This zone is called "puna." This name comes from a word in the Quechua language meaning "unpopulated land."

In northern Peru, another layer of vegetation may rise above the grass cover. This higher layer is more scattered and is characterized by the presence of *Puya raimondii*. This is a treelike bromeliad, which is similar to the giant senecios and the giant *Espeletia* plants. It reaches a height of 26 to 32 feet (8 to 10 m).

In this environment at an elevation of about 13,124 feet (4,000 m), the seasonal climatic variations are considerable. The daily temperature variations are also extreme. La Quiaca is an Argentine city near the border with Bolivia. This city is located at an elevation of about 11,480 feet (3,500 m). At La Quiaca, there is a 122°F (50°C) difference between the yearly high and low temperatures. Meanwhile, at Quito in Ecuador, which has an elevation of almost 9,845 feet (3,000 m), the range between annual highs and lows does not exceed 70°F (21°C). In the puna environments, the temperature during the day easily reaches 100°F (38°C), while the humidity drops to desert levels, which means less than 30 percent. During the night the temperature falls quickly to under 32°F (0°C).

The soil of the puna is deep and black down to about 3 feet (1 m). The top layer, however, is subject to rapid drying. Farther into the puna, there is a greater concentration of xerophyte plants. These are plants that tolerate dry conditions. An arid, semidesert type of vegetation is found in this area. The vegetation is characterized by spiny, juicy plants. They include prickly pear cacti, pincushion cacti, various paper-spined cacti, and cacti of the *Oroya* genus. The paper-spined cacti are thickly covered with long, white hair. The hair keeps water loss at an extremely low level.

The only trees that grow in the puna belong to the genus *Polylepis*. This is the genus of the rose family. They are called "quenoas" by the Peruvians and are found at elevations up to 14,765 feet (4,500 m). No other trees in South America are able to grow at such high elevations. The *Polylepis* trees are not very tall and resemble shrubs more than trees. Their wood is reddish and covered by grayish bark.

ANIMALS OF THE ANDES

Animals are not easy to find among the vast and varied landscapes of the Andes. They are spread out in the desert areas and alpine meadows. They are hidden and protected by adaptations to the wind, the cold, and the sun. In addition, they may take refuge in the thick, green forests. Each of the multiple habitats of the Andes has its own animal populations. Several of these animals are so typical that they have almost become symbols of South America.

Andean Hummingbirds

Among the forest animals inhabiting the slopes of the Andes, the hummingbirds are perhaps the most beautiful. They are characteristic of many different South American environments. Because of their size, coloring, eating habits and type of flight, they represent a rather special group of vertebrate animals. Their eating habits have earned them the nickname "insect-birds." It is possible to see them around the open vegetation near the mountain streams or on the edges of clearings with flowering plants. The hummingbirds move among the flowers like green wasps. They remain motionless for a moment in front of a flower while inserting their slender beaks into the flower. Then they dart off to another flower. Like winged insects, hummingbirds are able to hover in the air by rapidly beating their wings. They feed on nectar. Due to their incredible speed, they have little or no fear of predators.

Meyer di Schaunsee recently authored two accurate guides to the birds of Colombia and Venezuela. He listed at least 1,556 species of hummingbirds. This number represents 56 percent of all the bird species of South America. The hummingbirds are spread throughout the Andes. They are found from the tropical forests to the paramos. Their adaptability and extraordinary efficiency in flying have allowed these birds to occupy numerous ecological niches (smaller areas within a habitat). During this process, they have shown exceptional evolutionary success. This evolution occurred before the Western civilizations interfered with their environments. A large part of the natural habitats of South America have been altered, eliminated, or disturbed. Millions of square miles of tropical forest were burned or replaced by cultivated crops. Even large areas of the mountain forest and the cloud forest were destroyed. If the soil is not protected by a cover vegetation, after several years erosion begins to take place. As a consequence, the land is soon transformed into a desert.

Opposite page: The Peruvian puna is the ideal habitat for the vicuna. This animal lives between elevations of 11,480 and 18,860 feet (3,500 to 5,750 m). Territorial groups of vicunas can occasionally be seen in small valleys or depressions where water collects in pools. A territorial group consists of an adult male and a varying number of females and young. The group rarely numbers more than twenty. The photograph shows a group with young. A second social group is made up of unmated males that are not territorial. These adult males may gather in groups of up to one hundred individuals. The vicuna is the only hoofed animal characterized by continuously growing lower incisor teeth. With these teeth, the vicuna feeds on the oldest and most leathery grasses as well as mosses and lichens. The puna of the plateaus of central Peru is the preferred environment for the vicuna, although the species is distributed from Ecuador to northern Chile and Argentina.

The map indicates the areas of distribution of hummingbirds. The numbers indicate the amount of the different species found in each area. Within each zone, the distribution of species varies with the geography of the zone.The illustration on the opposite page shows several of the most widespread hummingbirds of the Andean environments. *From left to right and from top to bottom:* crimson topaz; *Calothorax lucifer;* ruby-throated hummingbird; *Lesbia victoriae;* Trochilus anna; sword-billed hummingbird; *Augastes maccheleus;* giant hummingbird.

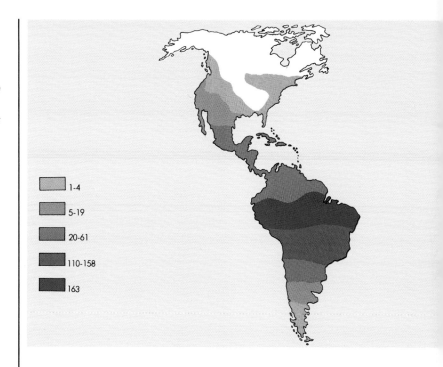

1-4

5-19

20-61

110-158

163

The hummingbirds are among the animal species that are most drastically affected by this rapid and destructive advance of civilization. For each square mile of destroyed forest, thousands of animals are lost. When the natural environment vanishes, the species that previously inhabited that area can no longer survive. Many hummingbirds are presently listed as endangered species.

Hummingbirds are present everywhere, but especially in the forest. A brilliant green color dominates the hummingbird's plumage, particularly on its back. This evidently acts as camouflage. When a hummingbird remains motionless on a branch, it blends in extremely well with the green foliage. It would be difficult to describe all the species of hummingbirds that live in the Andes.

One excursion to the forests of the Cordillera de Merida would provide the visitor with the opportunity to observe several of the most beautiful species. One example is the crimson topaz. This bird is characterized by a long, forked tail, a topaz green throat, and a bright, scarlet body. The small Incan collared hummingbird is green and white. The hummingbirds of the genus *Coeligera* have green, bronze, and violet coloring. The sword-billed hummingbird has a very long beak. The hummingbird *Aglaiocerus kingi* has a beautiful tail with green and blue feathers. It lives in the

vegetation band of the cloud forest where it can be easily seen darting over the low shrubs.

This apparent resemblance to insects is significant. The hummingbirds, and the African sunbirds represent a particular evolutionary line of birds. A few million years ago, they began to occupy habitats that had previously been the domain of insects only. The insects had acted as pollinators and nectar-eaters.

Hummingbirds are among the smallest vertebrates. The tiniest hummingbirds weigh about 0.07 ounce (2 grams). The largest, called the giant hummingbird, weighs 0.7 ounce (20 g). Unfortunately, little is known of the evolutionary history of these colorful birds. The reason for this lack of knowledge is the absence of fossil remains due to the environment. These environments include forests, thickets, and grasslands. Furthermore, the hummingbirds are so tiny and delicate that only exceptional circumstances could create conditions suitable for the conservation of their remains over long periods of time.

Numerous biological problems must be solved by such a tiny, warm-blooded organism whose flight consumes a tremendous amount of energy. A warm-blooded animal must constantly maintain a high body temperature. The tremendous speed of wing flapping involved in a humming-

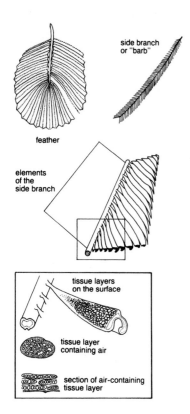

feather

side branch or "barb"

elements of the side branch

tissue layers on the surface

tissue layer containing air

section of air-containing tissue layer

The most amazing characteristic of the tiny hummingbirds is their brightly colored plumage. This peculiarity is due to the particular structure of the feathers. The feathers contain tissues that hold air. These tissue layers absorb varying amounts of light that is reflected on the plumage. How much is reflected depends on the amount of air the tissues contain. This causes a variation in the coloring.

bird's flight requires many calories. Thus, the humming-birds must feed almost constantly. Nectar is the ideal food because it has a high sugar content. It is not true, as was once believed, that hummingbirds feed exclusively on nectar. They also need a considerable amount of protein. Hum-mingbirds habitually prey on the small insects that are found on flowers, such as flies, small bees and wasps, and spiders. They capture the insects with the tips of their sticky tongues. An insect diet is common among the species of Andean hummingbirds that live at high elevations. At these elevations, there are not as many flowers available as in the forests.

Hummingbirds do not live exclusively in warm cli-mates. Several species of the genus *Oreotrochilus* are found in the high, cool mountains. The mountain hummingbirds are a little less colorful than their forest relatives. The giant hummingbird lives in the mountains. It is the size of a swift, but it is characterized by the typical long beak of the hummingbirds. With their beauty and unusual appearance, the hummingbirds could not have escaped Darwin's notice. In the 1800s, Darwin noted that these birds consumed a sizable amount of insects.

Several hummingbird species have been observed at elevations of up to 16,405 feet (5,000 m). On the plateaus where the bushes and the flowers are rare, the mountain hummingbirds generally do not build nests among plants. The nests are built on the eastern face of a crag in order to benefit from the warmth of the first rays of the morning sun. Over 75 percent of the nests are built on the eastern side of these crags. The birds that are not able to occupy this preferred habitat nest among the bushes at the base of the rocks. Females are responsible for building the nest.

In the paramos, the flower-piercers are the ecological equivalent of the hummingbirds. These nectar-eating birds are characterized by specialized feeding habits. The beauti-ful colors of the blue flower-piercer are similar to the dra-matic hues of the hummingbirds. Unlike the hummingbirds and the sunbirds, the flower-piercers have never served as pollinating agents for the flowers they feed on. To reach the nectar of the flower, they pierce the walls of the floral cup with their sharply-pointed beaks. They extract the nectar with rapid movements of the tongue. This behavior can be considered parasitic as it benefits only the bird and does not contribute anything to the plant. The nectar is produced by the flower in order to attract pollinating agents. Unlike

Pictured is a panoramic view of the prairie that characterizes the high-elevation zone of the Nahuel Huapi National Park in Argentina. The constant aridity and the low temperatures typical of these Andean environments produce unfavorable conditions for the animal populations. The few animals that inhabit these environments have special adaptations, such as thick plumage or hair. Some find shelter in underground dens or in cavities. The daily behaviors and routines of some are dependent upon the warmth of the sun's rays.

insects, hummingbirds, and sunbirds, the flower-piercers take advantage of this production without giving any service in return.

Meadowland Inhabitants

The Andean meadows have a unique ecology due to the unusual climatic conditions of the high-elevation plateaus. At an elevation of 13,125 feet (4,000 m), the characteristic bushes of the puna cover the ground as far as the eye can see. This environment is poor but does not lack the necessary elements for animal life. The seeds of the numerous grasses guarantee an abundant production of food. The constant aridity and the low night temperatures are important factors in determining the types of animals that can live in this area. The absence of trees and shrubs deprives numerous species of the necessary materials to build their nests and shelter and to hide from predators.

These environmental conditions are highly "selective" for reptiles and amphibians. This means that these factors determine, or select, which species will live here. Only those that evolve special adaptations are able to survive under these conditions.

A female marsupial frog is shown. This photograph was taken at an elevation of 11,480 feet (3,500 m) in an Ecuadoran paramo environment. This amphibian has the unusual habit of carrying its eggs in a skin pouch on its back. The small frogs that hatch from this pouch are either already in the adult stage or are tadpoles that must continue their development in the water.

The skin of amphibians is very sensitive to the sun and dries out easily. Thus, most reptiles have not succeeded in colonizing these habitats. Almost all of the few species of frogs and toads present in the Andean meadows have become exclusively aquatic. They are found only in the permanent lakes. On the shores of Lake Titicaca, the loud and melodious calls of the Pleuroderma cinerea, one of the most common toads, can be heard.

The number of reptile species is also very limited, although they are more adapted than the amphibians to withstand the dry conditions. Like the amphibians, the reptiles are cold-blooded and have great difficulty in moving about in cooler temperatures. The low atmospheric pressure at these high altitudes creates great daily drops in temperature. Most reptiles cannot withstand this.

The few reptile species that do live in this region are very specialized. One example is the smooth-throated lizard. This lizard is found only in sloping zones with a southern exposure. It has been found up to an elevation of 16,405 feet (5,000 m). There it warms itself by basking in the sun on the rock walls. At high elevations, the rock walls form

An example of a mouth-breeding frog, *Rhinoderma darwini*, was photographed at Concepcion, Chile. This small frog lives in the forests of Chile and southern Argentina. It measures about 1 inch (2.5 cm) and has a long piece of skin extending from the snout. After mating, the male remains near the eggs. When the developing organisms start to move around inside the eggs, the male inserts them inside its large throat sac. After three weeks, the young leave the sac either as small frogs in adult form or as tadpoles that must further develop in the water.

small climatic pockets. These pockets are warmer than the surrounding areas. Numerous invertebrates such as insects also inhabit these warmer microclimates. These invertebrates make up the diet of the smooth-throated lizards.

The birds and mammals of the high Andes are protected from the cold by feathers and coats of hair. They manage to survive in this treeless and shrubless environment by using burrows and holes in which to lay eggs or raise their young. Not surprisingly, rodents have established a large ecological niche in this grassland environment. They burrow dens deep underground where they shelter their young from the severe climate.

The rustling sound made by the Bolivian field mouse as it runs through clumps of ichu grass is often heard on the plateau. This rodent is the size of a large vole, or stocky rat. Its coat of hair is spotted with black. The short tail limits its heat loss. This rodent has acquired daytime habits in order to protect itself from the cold night temperatures. Its den consists of tunnels 65 to 100 feet (20 to 30 m) long dug in the subsoil to a depth of about 1 foot (30 cm).

The most characteristic rodents of this environment are the chinchillas, the mountain viscachas, and the cavies.

This mountain viscacha differs in appearance and behavior from its relative that inhabits the grassy expanses of the pampas. The mountain viscacha is as large as a hare and has strong hind legs. It hops about in search of food. This animal is one of the few mammals that manages to live above 13,120 feet (4,000 m) of elevation. It takes refuge inside cracks in rocks from the strong midday sun and the cold night temperatures.

At one time, the chinchilla was on the verge of extinction due to extensive hunting. The fur of this animal is highly valued. Fortunately, the Europeans discovered that it was easy to raise these animals in captivity. Since then, hunting of the chinchilla has decreased. In 1924, a man named Chapman brought eleven chinchillas to the United States and started raising the species. All of the chinchillas now raised in captivity throughout the world have descended from those few specimens.

The cavy, or guinea pig, is one of the oldest mammals to have been domesticated. Its remains have been found in pre-Incan archaeological sites dating back six thousand years. The Andean cavy's range extends to an elevation of 13,780 feet (4,200 m). It lives in small groups of five to ten individuals that occupy vast and complex underground dens. The Andean cavy is nocturnal or active at night. It leaves its hideout at dusk and follows well-established trails through the vegetation to reach its feeding locations. It eats different types of grasses, shoots, and seeds. The cavies represented one of the main food sources for the Andean

The process by which two guanacos recognize each other is different depending upon the age of the animals. The behavior between two adults is different from that between an adult and a young guanaco or between a male and a female. *From left to right and from top to bottom:* The points where guanacos are sniffed for recognition, marked by numbers that correspond to the smelling sequence; submissive or surrendering pose of a young guanaco *(at right)* when meeting an adult; fighting between two adults; courtship between a male *(at right)* and a female.

people. Even today, cavies are still raised for human consumption. In certain parts of South America, it is not unusual to be offered a dish containing cavy meat.

The numerous rodents represent an abundant food source for many predators. These include small falcons, owls, and the long-legged savanna fox. The savanna fox resembles a jackal.

One of the larger animal species inhabiting the paramo is the mountain tapir. It is of average size, with a stocky body and woolly hair. The mountain tapir is seen infrequently. The only South American bear species is the spectacled bear. It inhabits the Andean grasslands. However, it normally lives at lower elevations in environments other than tropical forests.

The Guanaco and the Vicuna

Among the large herbivores that arrived in South America from the north, the camel-like animals are now the most widespread. The guanaco spread as far as the plains of Patagonia. The vicuna is typical of the Peruvian puna. Two other species are known only in the domestic state. One is the llama, which served as a beast of burden for the ancient

Llamas, both domestic and wild, form groups that are considerably larger than the groups of their relatives, the guanacos and the vicunas. The photograph shows a long file of llamas following a trail in the Cordillera Real, in Bolivia, at an elevation of 14,760 feet (4,500 m). The llama has an irregular distribution area. It is found most often in southern Peru, Bolivia, western Argentina, and the puna of Atacama in Chile. It generally lives between elevations of 8,200 and 14,760 feet (2,500 to 4,500 m). This altitude is in between the habitats of the vicuna and the guanaco, which also live at sea level. The llama is now raised as a domestic animal.

Peruvians. It is larger and heavier than the guanaco. It reaches a weight of up to about 310 pounds (140 kg), compared to the guanaco's 198 pounds (90 kg). The second domestic species is the alpaca, which is smaller than the llama. The alpaca has been selectively bred for the quality of the wool it produces. Its hair is either brown, black, or white. This animal reaches a length of up to 20 inches (50 cm). In the era of the Incan empire, this animal was reserved for the exclusive use of the king.

Today, the guanaco survives in parks in the Andean region. Until the beginning of this century, this animal could

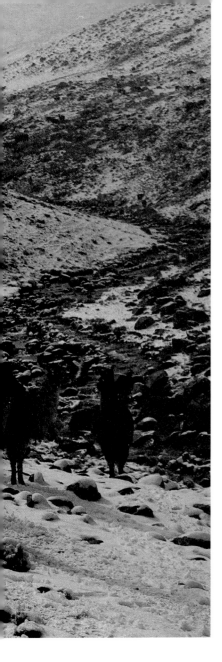

be spotted even from far away on the dry pampas. It has an elegant profile with long legs and neck. Its ears are pointed and erect, and its coat is woolly and frayed. The guanaco normally lives in small groups of thirty individuals. However, in the desolate plains of Patagonia, it occasionally gathers in groups of one hundred or more.

The shrill, neighing sounds of the guanacos indicate their presence long before they are spotted. These sounds are their cries of alarm. Guanacos generally flee in single file as soon as an intruder approaches. As they do so, their gait appears to be very light and slow. Normally, every group of guanacos posts a lookout, preferably from higher ground. This sentry watches motionless over the landscape and calls out to the group at the first sign of danger. As the alarm signal is given, the animal seems to be showing its healthy physical condition to the potential predator. At this point, the predator may conclude that this prey would be difficult to catch.

Guanacos live in groups made up of many females and a dominant adult male. The females are accompanied by the young born that year. Males fight each other fiercely in order to conquer a territory and dominate a group of females. They neigh loudly and bite during their fights. It is not rare to see large males with their coats covered by deep scars from such mating-season behavior. Between August and September in the reserves where they are most numerous, the males sound their shrill cries. The cries soon change into a low, rumbling sound.

The vicunas are smaller than the guanacos. They have long, brown hair and are lightly colored under the chin. The vicuna is also highly territorial. William Franklin studied the social structure of this species in the Pampas Galeras reserve in Peru at an elevation of 13,125 feet (4,000 m). He found that a group consisted of six to thirty individuals. The grazing area of the group varies from 17 to 74 acres (7 to 30 hectares), depending upon the size of the group and the availability of edible plants.

The social order is rigidly ruled by the dominant male. The number of males in the group is kept at a low level. The young males are driven away before the age of six months. These young males are forced to roam in nomadic, loosely structured herds. This is the case unless they are able to successfully fight a territorial male or dominate a group of young females. Young females are driven away by adult females of a group when the time for giving birth nears.

GALÁPAGOS ISLANDS

The author Herman Melville was enchanted by the Galápagos Islands during his vagabond travels around the world. To the author, these islands symbolized the harshness and cosmic indifference of nature with regard to human beings. Some of Melville's writing is filled with a sense of estrangement and alienation from nature as it exists on the islands. It was as if these islands represented another world, an upside-down image of existence.

An Overview

In the past, the hardship experienced by the sailors who visited these islands was largely due to the difficulty in finding sources of fresh water to supply their expeditions at sea. For the greater part of the year, the lowland zones of the islands are arid. Even during the rainy season, water does not gather in pools or ponds that are easily reached.

The islands are covered by dark, volcanic rock formed from hardened lava. Many small, sharp pieces of the lava rock resulted from the fragmenting action of the wind and rain. The volcanoes are not extinct, but are still somewhat active. Recently, frequent eruptions have occurred.

The archipelago or island group, is located at the equator about 620 miles (1,000 km) off the coast of Ecuador. It extends for about 186 miles (300 km) from east to west and almost that same distance from north to south. The total surface area of the land is 3,043 sq. miles (7,883 sq. km). The islands are connected to the South American continent by an underwater mountain chain called the Carnegie Ridge. They are also connected to Central America by the underwater Cocos Ridge. The Galápagos archipelago is composed of thirteen major islands and a number of smaller islands and islets. The islands are located above a relatively shallow underwater shelf.

The islands can be divided into two groups according to their age. The most ancient group is located over the high part of the underwater shelf in water that is 656 feet (200 m) deep. This group consists of small islands. For the most part, they follow a northwest-southeast line. Their names are Espanola, Santa Fe, the two Plazas, Baltra, Seymour, and the narrow northeastern strip of the island of Santa Cruz. The lava that has poured forth from their volcanoes is very acidic. The islands of this first group have a low, flat profile. The tableland (plateau) is composed of volcanic rock and steep reefs along the shores.

The greater part of the archipelago belongs to the

Opposite page: A colony of blue-footed boobies nests on Isabela, the largest island of the Galápagos Islands. The American writer Herman Melville described the shape of this island as looking like "jaws" that were about to crunch the smaller island of Fernandina. The young boobies in their light plumage are padded with fat reserves. At the end of their growth period, they are actually larger than their parents. These fat reserves are necessary in learning the difficult art of fishing when the young must fend for themselves. The blue-footed boobies are excellent divers, capable of fishing in shallow water without the risk of hitting bottom. Their cousins, the red-footed boobies, fish in the high seas. The parents must fly long distances in order to transport food to their young. The efficiency of the blue-footed booby in this regard explains why this species can raise two or three young. In comparison, the red-footed booby lays only one egg in each nest.

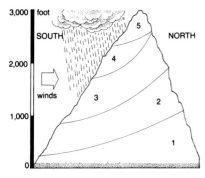

(1) shore zone and arid zone; (2) transition zone; (3) *Scalesia* zone; (4) *Miconia* zone; (5) grassland zone.

second group, which was formed more recently. It is made up of islands with small and large volcanoes that have gradually sloping sides. They are dotted with secondary volcanic cones. These islands are Fernandina, Isabela, Pinta, Marchena, San Salvador, San Cristobal, and the larger part of Santa Cruz. The volcanoes found here reach a maximum elevation of 5,600 feet (1,707 m) with the Wolf volcano on the island of Isabela. The volcanoes are topped with classic craters or, more often, with wide calderas. Calderas are older craters that have sunk down, growing extremely wide in the process. This site of complex volcanic phenomena makes the Galápagos an ideal place for the

Bottom: The volcanic nature of the Galápagos is evident in almost every detail of the landscape. Here, on the island of Bartolom, the circular remains of an eroded sunken crater can be seen in the foreground. Erosion of the crater was brought about by the action of the waves. Along the slopes of the coast, there are signs of recent lava flows. The nearby island of Santiago can be seen in the background. To the right is the low volcanic cone of Cerro Inn.

Opposite page: A simplified scheme of the vegetation zones of the island of Santa Cruz is provided. This scheme can be used as a model for the vegetation of the entire archipelago.

study of volcanoes and volcanic activities. As a whole, the islands have a rather dark appearance due to the black-and-gray tones of the lava rock.

The landscape is characterized by physical features such as lagoons located behind sand dunes and mangrove trees. The lagoons were formed by perfectly circular craters. Other typical features are sulphur deposits, run-off channels for lava flows, and lava fields. Only a few pioneering plant species succeed in growing on the lava fields. Numerous flamingos and sea lions share this landscape.

The Magic Islands

Melville described the Galápagos Islands as being cursed not only in a magical sense but also in a physical sense. The archipelago is cut by the equator. This creates an alternating pattern of a long dry season and a short humid season. Rainfall is very irregular. During the humid season, a strip of vegetation grows in areas otherwise characterized by bare shrubs and brush. Part of the islands' magical aspect was the difficulty in locating them on the nautical charts. This was due to the presence of seasonal ocean currents.

In 1574, mapmakers gave the islands a second name. They called them "Islas de los Galápagos," which derived from a peculiarity of their animal populations. In Spanish galapago means "turtle" or "tortoise." In the past, the giant Galápagos tortoises were extremely abundant on the islands. Their primitive appearance and slow, awkward movements gave a sense of unreality to the islands. There were also many dragon lizards. These reptiles are actually marine iguanas and land iguanas. Since 1832, the islands have been part of Ecuador. In 1892, on the occasion of the fourth centennial of the discovery of America, the Galápagos were renamed "Archipielago de Colon." This was done in honor of Christopher Columbus.

By then, however, the name *Galápagos* had already become famous. This was primarily due to Darwin's book of the account of the journey of the *Beagle*. The formulation of Darwin's theory of evolution is closely associated with the observations he made on the Galápagos. In particular, it was precisely the recognition of the different varieties and characteristics of the Galápagos tortoises on each island that led Darwin to reject the notion of the unchangeability of species. At that time, this notion was universally accepted as fact. The Galápagos and their animals are a classic case of the study of evolution.

A Particular Animal Community

It is not surprising that the Galápagos have become famous for the characteristics of their animals. There are many other areas of the world with interesting animals. And, of course, evolution has been going on, and still continues, in every part of the globe. However, on the Galápagos, a series of circumstances has arisen that makes the islands unique. The circumstances relate to their origin, age, and distance from the American continent. The islands are affected by the seasonal influence of a warm ocean current ("El Nino" from the north) and a cold current ("Humboldt" from the south). These currents cause unusual climatic conditions. The distance between the islands is far enough so that animals cannot interact frequently. However, the distance is close enough to allow a small amount of exchange between islands. Taken separately, each of these characteristics would be enough to make the Galápagos interesting from a zoological or evolutionary point of view. Taken together, these factors make the archipelago absolutely unique.

There is great interest in the animals of the Galápagos in spite of the fact that they are not very specialized creatures, nor are the species particularly showy or beautiful. In fact, the Galápagos have a small number of animal species. There are few mammals and no amphibians. Entire orders of birds and reptiles are absent, not to mention the invertebrate animals. However, it is precisely this scarcity that allows one to grasp the picture of evolutionary forces at work over time. For example, the thriving population of Galápagos tortoises was made possible by the lack of predatory land animals and competitors. In addition, the absence of woodpeckers enabled the finches to occupy an available ecological niche.

Origin and Colonization

The Galápagos are islands of completely volcanic origin. They are formed of basaltic rock. These islands rise over a vast submarine shelf that is not connected to the continental shelf. The age of the islands is estimated to be between 1.5 and 3 million years. However, they are young in respect to the origin of life on earth. When the Galápagos Islands emerged from the waters of the Pacific, the ancestors of humans were already walking erect and making tools in eastern Africa. Reptiles appeared over 200 million years ago and reached the peak of their population development

A pair of flightless cormorants nests. This species lives in an environment lacking ground predators. The flightless cormorants have developed excellent swimming skills. As a consequence, this species has lost the capacity to fly, and their wings have been reduced to simple stubs. Both male and female brood the eggs and care for the young. They have a curious system of taking turns. When one of the parents arrives to relieve the mate, it must bring a symbolic gift. This may be a strand of algae, a small piece of wood, or a starfish. If the arriving bird does not bring a gift, it is treated badly and does not get the opportunity to brood the eggs. This ritual is perhaps used to recognize the partner.

Opposite page: Courting among cormorants is a rather complicated affair. It assures the two partners of a solid tie as a pair. *From top to bottom:* The first phase occurs in the water with the two partners swimming, necks folded into an S-shape; the male swims toward the shore "guiding" the female; the male tosses its head to the rear and then bows in front of the female. These demonstrations can be repeated for a period of hours. Several elements of this courtship continue even after the building of the nest and the hatching of the eggs.

Another peculiarity of the Galápagos is the fact that penguins live there even though the islands are located at the equator. The presence of these birds is made possible by the low temperature of the sea. This results from the cold Humboldt Current coming from the southern regions. This current must have carried the ancestors of the modern Galápagos penguins to the archipelago. After arriving, they adapted to the new conditions and formed a new species in the process. The Galápagos penguins are the smallest existing penguins. This is due to the warmer environmental conditions of these islands. In the cold climates, a large body size is advantageous as it reduces the loss of heat. This is a major factor for survival in the cold climates. In the mild climate of the Galápagos, there was no selective pressure to evolve a larger body. The result was the present small size of the penguins.

during the age of the dinosaurs. That occurred about 150 million years ago.

Thus, the Galápagos were not the site of major evolutionary events. In other words, new classes, orders, or families of animals did not originate there. The islands are too recent for these events to have taken place. On the other hand, there are very interesting phenomena of small evolutionary change among the few species present on the Galápagos Islands. For example, there was the late evolution of the Galápagos tortoise. In the rest of the world, the giant tortoise had already reached its widest range of habitat millions of years before. Sixty million years ago, the giant tortoise *Triassochelys dux* dragged its one-ton body all across present-day Europe. Its shell was surprisingly similar to the shell of the Galápagos tortoises. The pre-Europe variety became extinct because of predators and competition with mammals. Similar tortoises are found only in one other place—on the atoll (a ring-shaped coral island) of Aldabra in the Indian Ocean.

To understand the history of the animal and plant population of the Galápagos, it is necessary to know about the relationship between the archipelago and the South American continent. There are three theories regarding this

The Galápagos Islands are inhabited by a native subspecies of the California sea lion. The California sea lion is found in the Sea of Japan, on the northwestern coast of Mexico, and on the southern coast of California. Like the Galápagos fur seal, the California sea lion has a social organization based on a harem. The harem is a group of females controlled by a dominant male. The unmated males live outside the territories of the dominant males. The main activity of a dominant male is that of keeping away the other adult males from the females within its territory. The dominant male also prevents playful cubs from venturing too far from shore, where sharks are a constant danger.

relationship. One is the theory of continuity. The second proposes that the Galápagos and South America were at one time located next to each other. The third theory is that the Galápagos are oceanic in origin.

According to the theory of continuity, the archipelago was originally connected to the continent. However, an analysis of the plants, animals, and rock formations shows that this is highly improbable. The plants and animals are mainly of an island type, even though they are of a definite South American origin. It is difficult to explain why only a few species survive in the Galápagos in comparison to the richness of the South American plants and animals. Only a particularly selective catastrophe, capable of wiping out some major groups of plants and animals and not others, could explain this fact. This type of catastrophe seems highly unlikely.

The second theory proposes that the Galápagos were not connected with the continent but were near it. This proximity was possible because of a peninsula that stretched out from the islands toward the continent. It is further theorized that the peninsula later sank into the ocean. This theory would explain why many continental species of plants and animals have the characteristics of island dwellers.

This theory would also suggest a way that the islands had been colonized. It proposes that the sunken peninsula was only 30 miles (50 km) from the continent. Unfortunately, there is no geologic proof of this. The study of the ocean floor has not produced any substantial evidence of this despite the presence of the Cocos and Carnegie ridges.

The third theory, involving an oceanic origin for the Galápagos, was proposed by Darwin. He claimed that the islands arose from the sea following submarine volcanic activity. Some time later, they were populated by mobile species or by species that were carried there passively. Today, this theory is more accepted than the others. It is also supported by the makeup of the island plants and animals. It is imagined that the least mobile species were "ferried" across the ocean to the islands by floating materials that served as rafts. Actually, the drifting of large tree trunks and tangles of vegetation over long distances is a frequent phenomenon. The far-ranging seabirds and the winds also played an important role in passively carrying new species of plants and animals to the Galápagos.

And so, the theory that the Galápagos Islands originated as oceanic islands has found the most acceptance. The basis for this theory was proposed in the 1960s. It successfully solved the general problem of how colonization of the oceanic islands took place. The theory noted that the probability of the arrival of a new species on an island is related to the distance of this island from a land mass. An island's size is not an important factor in this theory.

Also important is a phenomenon that had been underestimated in biogeography. It concerned the local extinction of species. The smaller a population, the greater the chance that it will become extinct for whatever reason. Clearly, a small island has smaller populations of each species than a larger island. Thus, there exists a relationship between the surface area of an island and the number of species that inhabit it. The general rule seems to be that a population of a species doubles when the surface area of an island is increased by a factor of ten.

Soon after the beginning of the colonization process, there is a decrease in the number of new species that arrive. The higher the number of species already present, the less

Opposite page: Expanses of black lava are very common on the islands of the Galápagos. They are evidence of relatively recent and widespread volcanic activity. The most recently formed lava stretch often has a continuous surface. This surface will later be broken up by the action of pioneering plants and atmospheric agents. The photograph presents a view of the island of Bartolom as seen from the island of Santiago. The unmistakable isolated crag of Bartolom can be seen at the upper left.

The plant and animal species that have been imported by humans constitute a continuous threat to the native species of the Galápagos. In cases where native species are unable to compete with introduced species, the new species spread in an uncontrolled manner. This upsets the existing natural balances, which are the fruits of a long and unrepeatable evolutionary history. The elimination of many imported species has proved almost impossible. This photograph was taken along the slopes of the volcano Sierra Negra on the island of Isabela. The guava trees, imported and by now widespread on many of the islands, are slowly suffocating the native vegetation.

probability that the new arrivals will belong to new species. In addition, the number of available ecological niches is quickly reduced. This factor limits the maximum number of species in a given area.

Thus, as an island is gradually colonized, it fills with species. The rate of extinction increases and the rate of immigration decreases. This continues until a balance is reached. Knowing the rate of extinction and the number of species present at a given time, it is possible to calculate the number of years it takes an island to reach its balance.

Applying this model to the Galápagos, it can be seen why the number of species is relatively low. Since the

islands are small, they have a high rate of extinction. Because they are far from the continent, they have a low rate of immigration of new species. However, in the case of the Galápagos, it is necessary to keep in mind that volcanic catastrophes can further complicate this picture. For brief periods, the rate of extinction could be considerably increased.

Climate

The climate of the Galápagos is also unusual and contradictory. Since the archipelago is located at the equator, an equatorial type of climate could be expected. Instead, the climate is mild, and the ocean waters at certain times are chilly. This is the result of the cold Humboldt current coming from the Antarctic regions. In certain months, the air that is in contact with the water cools and becomes more dense. As a result, the warm, humid air is unable to rise. Because the moisture cannot condense at high altitudes, there is no precipitation. When the cold and humid lower air mass encounters the warmer air mass, an "inversion level" is formed. Fog forms at this level. There is occasional precipitation in the form of light drizzle. Consequently, the zones of the islands that are above this inversion level are completely arid. During this period, the average monthly precipitation does not exceed 0.8 inches (20 mm).

From December to March, the Humboldt current is displaced by the El Nino current. The current was given this name, which refers to the infant Jesus, because it arrives around Christmastime. This current is warmer and not as salty. It brings an increase in precipitation up to 6 inches (150 mm) per month. In certain years, the precipitation is greater. El Nino is very irregular in its movements. At times, it flows farther south than its normal route. This causes sharp changes in the temperature and the salinity (saltiness) of the ocean water.

A good example of the environmental stresses caused by El Nino occurred in 1982-1983. During this period, an uncommon increase in precipitation and temperature occurred. Various levels of the food chain were affected. Predatory birds temporarily abandoned several islands due to the sharp drop in the numbers of available prey. The marine iguanas, which are less mobile than the birds, were seriously threatened by a scarcity of the algae species they feed on. This was caused by the increased water temperature and the lower salinity.

Scalesia pedunculata

Scalesia incisa

Scalesia affinis

One of the most interesting evolutionary events of the Galápagos was the relatively recent transformation of herbaceous plants of the composite family into treelike forms. This process was favored by reduced competition with existing trees. The tree competitors are scarce on the islands because their heavy seeds could not be easily transported to the islands by passive methods (wind currents, for example). The composite plants of the genus *Scalesia* evolved from nonwoody plants into different treelike forms. The most common of these forms are shown in the illustration.

Vegetation

The same processes that have determined the unusual animal population have also affected the plants. The plants of the Galápagos have just as many unique and particular forms as the animals. Several years ago, 625 species and subspecies were counted on the islands. Of these, at least 36.5 percent were native. This was the result of isolation, as well as the process of spreading and adapting to available niches. About 250 species were introduced by humans. These plants are mostly concentrated near areas of human settlement.

The native plants reached the islands in different ways. Some arrived by sea, others with the wind, and still others were carried directly by animals. However, they all originated in South America.

The vegetation of the islands is influenced by various factors. These include the availability of water and its chemical qualities, the type of soil, and the elevation. Proceeding from the shore area to the high elevations of the volcanoes, several characteristic vegetation zones can be distinguished.

Along the shore, especially in the sandy areas or in the shallow lagoons with rock bottoms, the vegetation is conditioned by the salinity of the water. The dominant species consist of small trees, shrubs, and salt-tolerant plants.

In the bays and in the protected lagoons, there are vast, dense stands (groups of one dominant species) of red mangrove, white mangrove, and black mangrove trees. Alongside these trees, other aquatic trees such as the buttonwood, are found. On the land nearby, there are small shrubs and numerous species of the genus Sesuvium.

On the majority of islands, the shore zone is followed by an arid zone. Giant cacti dominate this landscape. The large prickly pear cacti are present as well as four species characteristic of the individual islands.

Trees and shrubs also grow in this zone. They are characterized by small leaves. Often, the leaves have evolved into spines to limit the loss of water through the leaf surfaces. Sometimes they grow from cracks in the lava. This is the case of the widespread incense tree. Other trees and shrubs are *Croton scouleri*, *Piscidia cartahagenensis*, and *Hippomane mancinella*, which produces small, applelike fruit. Despite their appetizing appearance, the fruit is quite poisonous. They contain a latex which is a milky, sticky sap that is also present in spurge plants.

The arid climate of the low-elevation zones has forced the island inhabitants to adapt to this existing condition. One of the most common adaptive strategies of Galápagos plants was the evolution of a thick, waxy layer surrounding the leaf surfaces. The size and number of leaves were also reduced. Many plants developed juicy tissues and spines. The plant of the genus *Sesuvium* is protected from heat by the color of its leaves. This color reflects the hottest part of the sun's radiation.

Following page: The whitish sweep of incense trees on the island of Santa Cruz is pictured. These trees remain dormant for long periods of time as a protection against the arid climate, so they usually have a dry appearance.

Above the arid zone, on the larger islands, there is a band of a humid type of vegetation. This is created by the presence of cloud banks and fog that maintain a cool, humid environment, even outside of the rainy season. This zone has been colonized by large, native, tree-shaped plants of the genus *Scalesia*.

Throughout the rest of the world, the plants of the composite family have not evolved past the herbaceous stage. However, in this environment, the herbaceous plants have evolved into a treelike form. This resulted from the lack of competition with the native tree species. The environment also proved particularly suitable for the coloniza-

tion of these plants. The Scalesia plants reached the Galá-pagos as an herblike plant. With time, however, it evolved into a treelike form.

The undergrowth is varied. It consists of shrubs, woody vines, bromeliads, numerous ferns, mosses, liverworts, and lichens. Most of these plants grow on the trunks, branches, and even the leaves of trees. On a small scale, this environment resembles the cloud forest of the Andes Mountains. It is characterized by clouds and extensive growths of epiphytic plants.

Higher in elevation are the forests of *Scalesia*. They are followed by a vegetation of relatively low shrubs. The prevailing shrub here is the caocaotillo (genus *Miconia*). It is 7 to 13 feet (2 to 4 m) tall with beautiful lance-shaped leaves. This tree produces clusters of small, purple flowers. This band of vegetation is called the "*Miconia* zone." It is particularly extensive on the island of Santa Cruz.

The uppermost zone of the large volcanoes is covered by meadows that are rich with ferns, grasses, and sedges. At this elevation, the precipitation is less than in the two lower zones. However, since the soil does not have good drainage, semipermanent pools of water are more frequent. Sphagnum moss is abundant. It forms thick mats soaked with water. Numerous sedges grow in this zone, including the native *Cyperus grandifolius*. There are also many plants of the grass and parsley family. It is interesting to note the adaptations of the horsetail plants. On the island of Isabela, they grow at elevations between 2,460 to 3,150 feet (750 to 960 m). In the Andes, however, they are normally found between 8,200 and 12,468 feet (2,500 to 3,800 m), but never below 4,590 feet (1,400 m).

This is also the zone of the large tree ferns, which can reach heights of 20 feet (6 m). The tree fern Cyathea weatherbyana has a trunk that reaches a diameter of 1 foot (30 cm). Its leaves are curved and can reach a length of up to 10 feet (3 m). It grows on the steep walls of the craters, in steep gorges, and in the cavities of the collapsed lava runoff channels.

The natural balance of the vegetation of the Galápagos is in serious danger. Presently, the islands host numerous plants that have been introduced by humans. These new plants represent a serious threat to the native plant species.

GALÁPAGOS TORTOISES

In days gone by, the ships of whalers and buccaneers anchored at bases in the Galápagos Islands. The whalers who navigated the Pacific Ocean routes were driven by the prospects of a fruitful hunt along the Humboldt current. The buccaneers sought to loot the Spanish ships that transported gold and silver back to the mother country. Though the islands were inhospitable in some ways, they definitely had some advantages. They provided a secure anchorage for ships. Sources of drinkable water were available to those who were able to locate them. Above all, there was a plentiful supply of good-quality, fresh meat that was easily obtained. This was the meat of the Galápagos tortoises, which at that time were numerous on all the islands. They provided protein and a particularly appetizing fat.

More than one traveler had remarked on the extraordinary abundance of the tortoises. This population density is not surprising. Given the same food resources, plant-eating reptiles in a given area will be more numerous than plant-eating mammals. The reptiles obtain the energy necessary for heating their bodies from the sun's radiation. The mammals, however, heat their bodies from the energy produced by food. Consequently, the mammals need more food resources.

Distribution and Behavior

Darwin disembarked on the Galápagos Islands in 1835 during his voyage aboard the *Beagle*. The naturalist was particularly struck by the giant tortoises. He noticed one detail that would later prove to be very important. This was that every island seemed to have its own particular variety of tortoises, characterized above all by the shape of the shell.

At that time, Darwin was still convinced of the unchangeability of the species. However, he had established the habit of keeping an open mind. He was very perceptive and not easily swayed by prejudiced thinking. Darwin could not rationalize that all of these tortoise varieties were created independently of each other. And why, he wondered, were these tortoise varieties not equally distributed around the globe, instead of just on these neighboring islands? The answer was that, over time, species undergo changes in relation to the environment in which they live. The basis of this evolution is also the basis for Darwin's great theory. In any given environment, the better-adapted individuals survive.

Opposite page: The Galápagos tortoise is the largest land animal on the islands. Its great size is evident when compared to the flycatcher perched on its back, awaiting the capture of insects. The photograph shows a subspecies with a dome-shaped shell.

The cacti of the species *Opuntia echios* greatly differ in shape from island to island. One is treelike with a thick trunk, while the other is bushlike. The Galápagos tortoise is the most important plant-eating animal on the islands. It is present only on the islands where this cactus has a treelike form. It is probable that the tortoises' browsing of this plant caused an evolution of its structure into plants that were less easily reached. This is confirmed by the fact that the young forms of this cactus have spines that are particularly hard (unlike the young forms of the bushlike types). This no doubt serves as protection from browsing animals. The technique used by tortoises to eat these cacti is quite interesting. After lowering the branches with its head, the animal breaks them by stamping on them. The tortoise then eats the plant parts on the ground.

Opuntia echios gigantea

Opuntia echios echies

The tortoises live both in desert zones and on plateaus with a humid climate. If water is available, they readily use it for drinking and will stay immersed in it for a large part of the day. They drink abundantly, submerging the front part of their heads and "pumping" the water. Immersing themselves in water acts to cool their bodies, and it helps to keep the mosquitoes away. Occasionally, during the dry season, the tortoises travel considerable distances to reach the humid zone. However, this is not always possible, given the various land formations and characteristics of the islands. In these cases, the tortoises drink from pools that form from the collection of rainwater. Or at night, they search for the dew that has collected in small basins between the rocks. These drinking locations are usually found at a certain elevation. To reach them, the tortoises move over trails that have been worn into the rocks by countless passages. These migrating routes have been used by generation after generation of tortoises over the course of thousands of years. The Spaniards used them to locate the scarce water resources on the islands.

During the long dry periods, the tortoises can use the water produced by the breakdown of their fat deposits. The tortoises also take advantage of the juicy pulp of the cacti.

The extensive eating of the cacti by tortoises has a considerable selective effect on these plants. The widespread cacti of the genus *Opuntia* grow low to the ground on the islands where the tortoises are not present. Furthermore, the spines of the young cacti are relatively soft on these islands. However, the *Opuntia* cacti on the islands where tortoises use them for water have evolved defensive features. These cacti have a treelike shape and a woody trunk. They grow away from the ground. Their young forms are well protected by hard spines. Over the course of evolution, the tortoises have developed adaptations in response to this. Their legs and neck have become longer and the part of the shell behind the head has been altered. This allows the tortoises to reach the softer parts of the cacti higher off the ground.

This recent evolutionary competition is quite evident. It is easily studied because of the small number of animals involved. Furthermore, the environment they inhabit is very simplified.

Continued hunting (although this hunting does not have a long history) of the Galápagos tortoises has drastically reduced their populations. It has also caused them to

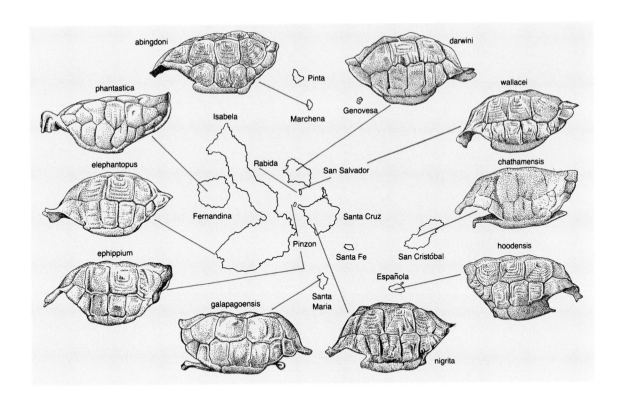

The diagram illustrates the islands inhabited by several of the most representative subspecies. Labels: abingdoni, phantastica, elephantopus, ephippium, galapagoensis, darwini, wallacei, chathamensis, hoodensis, nigrita. Islands: Pinta, Marchena, Genovesa, Isabela, Rabida, San Salvador, Fernandina, Santa Cruz, Pinzon, Santa Fe, San Cristóbal, Española, Santa Maria.

The main subspecies of Galápagos tortoises differ mainly in the form of their shells. The shell may be shaped either like a saddle or like a dome. The saddle-shaped shell allows the animal to browse on plants as high as 3 feet (1 meter) from the ground. This type of shell is common among the tortoise subspecies that inhabit islands characterized by low humidity and scarce grass. On these islands, tortoises feed primarily on cacti and bushes. It has been theorized that the saddle-shaped shell is the result of "evolutionary competition" between the tortoises and the cacti of the genus *Opuntia*. As these cacti evolved in height, the tortoises evolved the ability to browse higher off the ground. On the islands where the tortoises graze on grasses in the higher, humid zones, their shells have the dome-shaped form that is characteristic of all land tortoises. The various subspecies also differ from each other in the pattern of the shell. The diagram illustrates the islands inhabited by several of the most representative subspecies. It is clear that the evolution of different subspecies is mainly due to geographic isolation.

become extremely cautious and withdrawn. When Darwin landed on the island of Chatham (present-day San Cristobal), he encountered a strange world of "giants."

Today, however, on the islands where they are widely hunted, the sight or even the smell of humans is enough to scare them away. The most numerous populations are found in zones that are difficult to enter. Hunting them in these inconvenient areas is not economically rewarding. On Santa Cruz, in the high, humid part of the island, a large population of tortoises still survives. The tortoises in this zone number about two thousand. They are very shy. They belong to the subspecies Testudo elephantopus nigrita, which is native to the island. Substantial populations are also found on the islands of San Cristobal (subspecies chathamensis), San Salvador (subspecies darwini), and above all, on the island of Isabela. Isabela is formed by five impressive volcanoes (Wolf, Darwin, Alcedo, Sierra Negra, and Cerro Azul). It is possible that, in the past, these volcanoes formed independent islands. Each volcano is inhabited by a different subspecies of tortoise. These subspecies have been separated from each other to this day by the lava flows along the slopes of the volcanoes.

A Peaceful Pace of Life

The best place to observe the tortoises at ease in their natural environment is the crater and the slopes of the Alcedo volcano on the island of Isabela. The most numerous population of Galápagos tortoises live there. This is also the only population that has not suffered from hunting nor the predation of animals introduced by humans. More than three thousand tortoises of the subspecies vandenburghi make their home in this area. After a climb of about four hours, it is possible to observe their peaceful way of life.

The tortoises become active at the first light of dawn.

Several examples of the tortoise population (subspecies vandenburghi) of the volcano Alcedo on the island of Isabela are shown. The Alcedo population is the largest of all the islands of the Galápagos. The Galápagos tortoises are perfectly adapted to the arid climate. Nevertheless, when water is available, they readily use it for drinking, lowering the body temperature, ridding themselves of parasites, and avoiding mosquitoes.

However, until the sun gets quite high in the sky, these reptiles remain a little sluggish. Their main task is searching for food. Feeding a 660-pound (300 kg) body is no small feat. During the hottest part of the day, the tortoises browse in the shade. In this way, they avoid the danger of overheating. With their legs left outside of the shell and the head supported on one of the front legs, the tortoises rest in the manner of a dog. They become active once more when the temperature drops.

At dusk, during the more humid season, they return to the pools of mud where they have spent the night. The mud protects them from the lower night temperature, as well as from ticks and mosquitoes. Whatever the reason, the puddles and pools are highly sought after, and the tortoises compete for the privilege of occupying them. They strongly shove against each other, and the smallest tortoises are driven away. In order to limit their heat loss during the night, these small tortoises dig holes in the soil. In areas where there are predators that have been introduced by humans (dogs and pigs that have escaped into the wild), the tortoises have developed the habit of sleeping with the front part of their shell inserted in a dense bush.

Although it is quite humid, the tortoises need even more moisture than what is available in the air in order to regulate their body heat. When a storm approaches, they head toward the areas where the rainwater will form pools and puddles. This perhaps is a case of individual learning or of the passing of learned behavior from one individual to the next, generation after generation. These slow reptiles show considerable intelligence and a complete knowledge of their territory.

At times, grating and rhythmic bellowing sounds can be heard from the tortoises. These sounds are emitted by the males during the mating season. When the males encounter each other, they raise as high as possible on their legs while widely opening their jaws. They do not bite each·other, however. Occasionally they push each other until one of the rivals retreats. These fights are highly ritualized encounters.

The female selects a soft, dry location to lay the eggs. She digs a perfectly round hole with the hind legs. Ten to fifteen spherical, white eggs the size of billiard balls are laid in the hole. After depositing the eggs, the female covers the hole very carefully. A female tortoise normally lays eggs two or three times per season. The young are hatched after an incubation of four to six months. About 75 percent of the

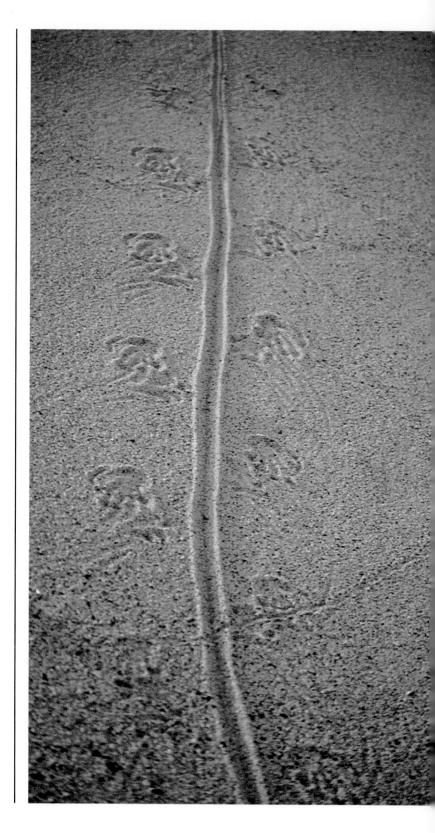

Pictured are the tracks of the slow passage of a tortoise in the sands of Bartolome Island. At one time, tortoises were on the verge of extinction on all of the islands. They were hunted by the whaling crews as a meat supply and by professional hunters for profit. The future of the most threatened tortoise subspecies is brighter. The Charles Darwin Research Station has been carrying out a special project to bring the tortoise population back up to earlier levels. The eggs of the turtles are hatched and raised in capitivity, and the young turtles are later released into the wild.

eggs that are laid hatch. Although the young tortoises grow rather quickly, they are particularly vulnerable to natural and introduced predators. The main natural predator of young tortoises is the Galápagos hawk. The young are subject to predation for a period of about three years. Sexual maturity is reached at about twenty-five years of age.

Conservation

The problem of saving the tortoises goes hand in hand with conservation of the environments of the Galápagos. Hunting has caused considerable damage to the tortoise populations. On several islands, the subspecies have become completely extinct. In 1936, the government of Ecuador passed a law aimed at protecting the animals of the Galápagos. However, this law was ignored for a number of years. It was not until 1954 that a policy of conservation was actually promoted. A biological station was installed. The station was inaugurated in 1961 on the island of Santa Cruz. It was named the Charles Darwin Research Station. The Ecuadoran government declared the archipelago a national park in 1959. Since the most representative and threatened species was the tortoise, the first task was that of protecting this animal and improving its situation. By this time, the threat to the survival of this species was no longer directly from humans. Rather, the threat was from the animals that had been introduced by humans. In the food chain of the native Galápagos animals, the tortoises represent by far the most important grazers. The introduction of more efficient, competing animals was extremely harmful.

Several animals introduced by humans represent the greatest danger for the tortoise populations. This is due to predation on the young tortoises or competition for the same food resources. The table shows the situation of various subspecies of the tortoise on the main islands.

| SUBSPECIES (TORTOISE) | INHABITED ISLAND OR PART OF INHABITED ISLAND | POPULATION | PREDATORS | | | | | | |
			pigs	dogs	cats	rats	goats	donkeys	cattle
Testudo elephantopus abingdoni	Pinta	unknown					x		
Testudo elephantopus chathamensis	San Cristóbal	500-700		x	x		x	x	
Testudo elephantopus hoodensis	Española	less than 50					x		
Testudo elephantopus ephippium	Pinzon	150-200				x			
Testudo elephantopus darwini	San Salvador	500-700	x			x	x	x	
Testudo elephantopus vandenburghi	Isbela (Alcedo Volcano)	3,000-5,000			x	x		x	
Testudo elephantopus becki	Isabela (Wolf Volcano)	1,000-2,000			x	x			
Testudo elephantopus microphyes	Isabela (Darwin Volcano)	500-1,000			x	x			
Testudo elephantopus guentheri	Isabela (Sierra Negra Volcano)	300-500							
Testudo elephantopus elephantopus	Isabela (Cerro Azuì Volcano)	400-600	x	x	x	x			x
Testudo elephantopus nigrita	Santa Cruz	2,000-3,000							

The situation of the known subspecies of tortoises in the Galápagos is shown on the graph. Human interference has destroyed or endangered almost all of the subspecies. Unfortunately, when a population, species, or subspecies is destroyed, something absolutely irreplaceable is lost. When a species disappears, the rich genetic information it carries with it is also lost forever. Even if species are destined to disappear sooner or later, it is a heavy responsibility for humans to directly play a role in their extinction. Sometimes this is only caused by greed, ignorance, or indifference.

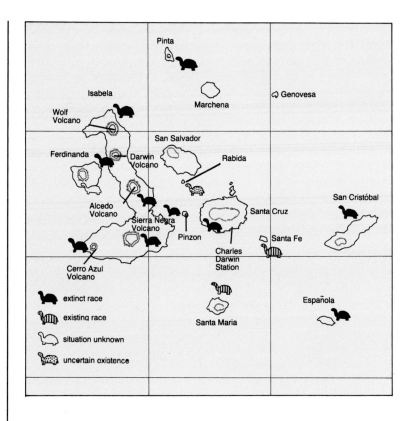

The goats in the wild were not so dangerous since their numbers could be easily controlled. The campaign to eliminate the wild goats met with some success. Thus, an introduced plant-eating species was kept from extensively competing with the tortoises. The real danger to the tortoises comes from the introduced animals that prey on the newly hatched and young tortoises. These animals include dogs and cats that have escaped into the wild. They are well adapted and widespread. They have found ecological niches that were previously empty. Domestic pigs also became wild. Their numbers have been increasing considerably in the open environments of the islands. While the populations of wild dogs, cats, and pigs can be somewhat controlled, it is difficult to eliminate them entirely. This is especially the case with the dogs, which have become very cautious and difficult to catch.

Rats have also invaded several of the islands. They cannot be completely eliminated nor can their numbers be controlled by selective killing methods. Rats prey on the eggs and young of the tortoises and also cause severe damage to the environment.

The beautiful swallow-tailed gull is another native species of the Galápagos Islands. This is the only species of gull that hunts at night. The reasons for this unusual habit are probably due to its pesky neighbors, the magnificent frigate bird and the great frigate bird. These two birds are specialized in taking away fish that are captured by smaller birds. The nocturnal habits of the swallow-tailed gull could have evolved in order to avoid daytime thefts of its food.

The project promoted by the Darwin station to save the most threatened tortoise subspecies was based on a simple idea. The tortoise eggs were collected and hatched in captivity at the biological station. After reaching a certain age, the young tortoises were released to the natural habitat of their original islands. This later release prevents the young tortoises from being preyed on during the most critical stage of their development. It is quite difficult to introduce birds and mammals that have been born in captivity into the wild. However, this is easily achieved with reptiles.

The short-term problem of the survival of the most threatened subspecies was thus solved. However, there still remains the long-term problem of reestablishing favorable environmental conditions. The introduction of certain new species upset the natural balance of the Galápagos Islands. It is quite clear that a management program that is solely oriented toward conserving the most threatened species is no longer enough. What is needed, rather, is an active management policy capable of straightening out situations that are almost completely out of balance.

DARWIN'S FINCHES

Of all the animals of the Galápagos, one would not guess that the finches would most inspire the imagination of a visitor or a biologist. When Darwin came to the islands, he was initially more impressed by the tortoises and the iguanas than by the finches. The large reptiles with their ancient, primitive forms made him feel closer to the mysterious event of the creation of an organism.

However, upon closer observation, Darwin noticed that the Galápagos finches were extraordinarily interesting. It was evident that the entire group of Galápagos finches had similar physical features and behavioral traits. All finches have a dark plumage and short tails and are small in size. They display territorial behavior and mate with only one partner. During the courtship period, the males offer gifts of food to the chosen female. Their nests are round. However, Darwin clearly identified many different species of finches based largely on the differences in their beaks.

It seemed that the "creative force" that Darwin strongly sensed in the Galápagos Islands created the various forms for the finches' beaks. Among the finches, Darwin noticed beaks that strongly resembled the beaks of the hawfinch, flycatcher, starling, blackcap warbler, and parrot. The existence of numerous unoccupied ecological niches gave this species the opportunity to develop into different forms.

Origin and Evolution

To get a look at the Galápagos finches is rather simple. Like most other native Galápagos animals, the finches do not fear humans. Several finch species can be observed in the same habitat, such as in the stands of tree cacti facing the bay of Accademia, on the island of Santa Cruz. The species that can be seen together here are *Geospiza magnirostris* (the large ground finch), *Geospiza fortis*, *Geospiza fuliginosa*, *Geospiza scandens*, and *Certhidea olivacea* (the warbler finch). To observe the various species, one need only offer them some food, even out of the hand. By offering them grains of rice, one can observe the different capabilities of the beaks of various species as they feed.

Darwin suggested that one single species of South American ground finch had originally reached the Galápagos Islands. He proposed that all of the other Galápagos finches successively evolved into different forms from this original species. Darwin's perception was later confirmed by the research of the ornithologist (bird scientist) David Lack. Lack suggested that a South American finch species

Opposite page: The Galápagos finches (or Darwin's finches) had an important influence on Darwin's formulation of the theory of evolution by natural selection. The phenomenon of the adaptation of these finches has been extensively studied. These birds are descendants of a ground-dwelling ancestor genus that originated in South America. They later evolved into forms characterized by unique beaks. For example, *Geospiza fortis* is able to crush the seeds of many plants. The finches have been able to occupy a variety of available ecological niches.

had arrived in the Galápagos possibly transported by a hurricane because finches have only modest flying abilities.

This species then colonized an island. In a relatively short time, a new population developed. This population had both predictable and unpredictable characteristics in respect to their South American origin. At least three factors account for the differences between the original and the later species. First, as a rule colonization is brought about by a few individuals that are "randomly" taken from the original population. These individuals, and thus their descendants, are not an average representation of the species to which they belong. Rather, they are only a small slice taken at random. This is called the "founder effect." Secondly, the local environmental conditions operate as a selective mechanism. This can have far-reaching effects over time. Thirdly, small populations are greatly affected by "genetic drift" (the random fluctuation of gene frequencies from generation to generation). This impulse to change is a haphazard occurrence and is not due to selection.

From the first island, the finches moved to colonize other islands. With each island, the population evolved into different local forms. This was favored by the low mobility of the birds. This low mobility prevented the easy mixing and breeding with other populations on other islands.

The differences in the tortoise varieties can give us an idea of the evolutionary forces that lead to change. The finches reproduce very rapidly. Therefore, their evolution into different forms has occurred at a faster rate than that of the tortoises. Thus, the finches plainly demonstrate how the evolutionary forces can produce a variety of species.

The accumulation of differences among various populations can be such that individuals belonging to different populations no longer mate with each other when they come into contact. This is the point at which one can say with certainty that a new species has evolved. However, this does not indicate when the species was created. The populations that live in the same area (for example, an island) can be easily classified into different species. However, it is more difficult to classify the species when the populations inhabit different areas.

There are no doubts about the Galápagos finches. Although they are not strong flyers, they are certainly more mobile than the land reptiles. Over time, the colonization and the evolution into different species have left some species more ancient than others. Occasionally, a recently

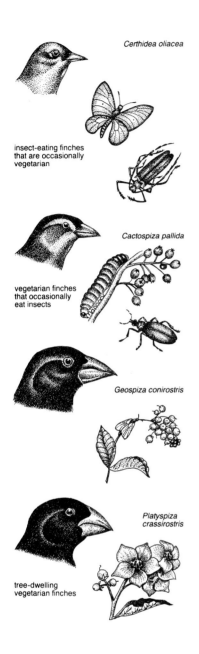

Certhidea oliacea

insect-eating finches
that are occasionally
vegetarian

Cactospiza pallida

vegetarian finches
that occasionally
eat insects

Geospiza conirostris

_Platyspiza
crassirostris_

tree-dwelling
vegetarian finches

The adaptive spreading of Darwin's finches was made easier by the number of unoccupied ecological niches on the Galápagos Islands. Given the geographic isolation, local populations of finches were able to evolve into distinct species. The present diversity in the shape of the beaks of the Galápagos finches is the result of a complex history of colonizations, adaptations, specializations, re-colonizations, and competition. What can be observed today is only a moment in time of this continuing evolution.

formed species migrates to a different island and mixes with an older species. When this occurs, the two forms do not unite through mating. Rather, they compete with each other for the same food sources. If niches are available, this competition eventually leads to the specialization of the two species. Thus, they become further diversified.

Recolonization and specialization occurred many times. Today, the Galápagos finches are classified into thirteen different species belonging to four genera. Up to ten different species of finches can be observed on the same island. Their specialization and adaptation to different niches allows them to live together on the same island. Their differences seem to be the result of intense competition between species for the available food resources.

It is difficult to find evidence of adaptive processes in the tortoise and iguana varieties. However, one can easily find this evidence in the finch beaks. The type of beak is directly related to an essential aspect of their way of life—their eating habits. The beak of _Geospiza magnirostris_ enables it to feed on large, hard seeds. The relatively big beak of _Geospiza fortis_ allows it to eat many types of moderately hard seeds. The beak of _Geospiza fuliginosa_ is adapted to eat tender seeds and insects. The finches of the genus _Camarhyncus_ have beaks that are specialized for closing tightly at the tips. These beaks are adapted for feeding on insects and tender seeds. The finches of the genus _Cactospiza_ have long, powerful beaks, specialized for eating insects and fruit. The finches of the genus _Platyspiza_ have beaks similar to those of parrots. This type of beak is capable of biting and chewing. It is adapted for eating buds, fruit, leaves, and seeds. Finally, the finches of the genus _Certhidea_ have thinner beaks. They are adapted exclusively for capturing insects.

Opportunism

The importance of unoccupied ecological niches is hard to measure. Once again the Galápagos finches provide help in understanding a process of nature. There are no woodpeckers on the islands although a niche is available for them. Woodpeckers feed on insect larvae that live in wood. This type of prey is abundant. However, a bird must be specialized in order to find the larvae and draw them out. The finch _Cactospizia pallida_ occupies this niche.

Occasionally, like the woodpecker, the finch will press its head against a tree trunk to listen for potential prey. Once

Proof of the importance of an available ecological niche for a species is the unusual adaptation of the *Cactospiza pallida* finch. This bird occupies the niche that is elsewhere occupied by woodpeckers, which are absent on the Galápagos. This finch feeds on insects that live in dead wood. Unlike the woodpeckers, its tongue is not long enough to capture prey. This problem is solved by using an instrument, usually a cactus spine, to take the place of the long tongue of the woodpecker *(top left)*. This behavior would probably not have evolved if the woodpeckers had been present in the same environment. The woodpeckers would have been more efficient in extracting the prey. Thus, the competition would have been too great. The illustration shows several phases of the extraction of an insect larva from a tree trunk by the *Cactospiza pallida* finch *(top right, bottom left, and bottom right)*.

the woodpecker locates the prey, it makes a hole and extracts the larva with the help of its long tongue. The *Cactospiza pallida* finch, however, does not have a long tongue. To capture its prey, it has taken a "shortcut" to evolution. Once it has made a hole in the tree, it flies to a nearby cactus and obtains a spine to extract the larva.

It has been observed that if this finch hunts in an area without cacti, it brings along an instrument in anticipation of its use. When spines are not available, this species makes its own suitable instrument.

Obviously, behaviors are more easily evolved over time than physical structures. However, the ability to use such instruments could hardly have been developed suddenly in *Cactospiza pallida*.

The capacity to use an instrument while searching for food must have been learned by trial and error. Playful behavior is an important role in this learning process. A young *Cactospiza pallida* finch experiments with grass stems that are too flexible and small twigs that are too large. Only with time and practice does the bird learn to correctly select the proper instrument.

It is facinating to observe this finch at work while dislodging insect larvae. These finches are found on the

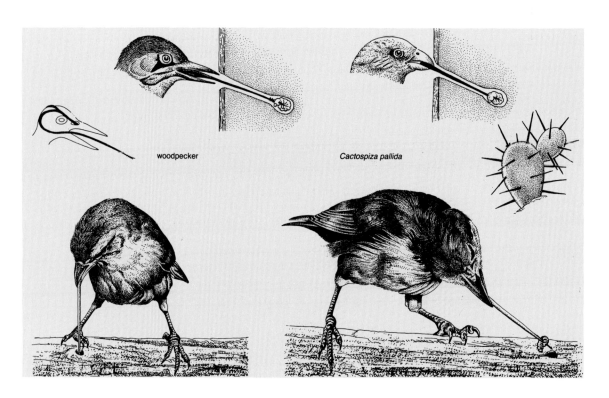

woodpecker

Cactospiza pallida

The Geospiza scandens finch, which has a medium-sized beak, is an opportunist. It will feed on seeds that are not excessively hard, fruit, the nectar of cactus flowers, and, when necessary, insects.

island of Santa Cruz in the cactus forest behind the bay of Accademia.

From an ecological standpoint, the Galápagos finches are opportunists ready to profit from any food possibility. This is confirmed by the relationship between the *Geospiza fuliginosa* finch and the tortoises and iguanas. The finches of this species eat the insect parasites of the tortoises and iguanas without being harmed.

This opportunism is also evident in *Geospiza difficilis*. On Santiago and Pinta, this finch lives in humid woods. It overturns leaves on the ground in search of insects and worms. On the islands of Darwin, Wolf, and Genovesa, it lives in the dry lowlands and feeds on seeds and cacti. It is clear that over a long period of time these different habits, together with geographic isolation, could give rise to different species. On the island of Wolf, *Geospiza difficilis* has been seen eating parasites off the bodies of booby birds while they remain motionless. This is an example of symbiosis, which is a relationship between two organisms that is helpful to both parties.

LAND AND SEA DRAGONS

The marine iguanas are the first animals that greet the visitor to the Galápagos Islands. These dark-crested reptiles can be seen lying motionless on the sharp, black rocks along the shore of the frothy sea. The effect of this scene is guaranteed to give the visitor the sensation that time has stopped here.

Actually, despite its appearance, the marine iguana is not a truly ancient reptile. This lizard is particularly adapted to an amphibian life. As a matter of fact, this species is perhaps the only truly marine lizard in the world.

Marine Iguanas

The marine iguana feeds mainly on ocean algae. It is an excellent swimmer, that is helped by the shape of its body and a tail that is flattened along the sides. The tail acts both as a rudder and for propulsion. While swimming, the legs are held next to the body. On the average, the marine iguana remains under the water for only a few minutes at a time to obtain food. However, it can remain under the water for over thirty minutes.

One problem that many marine animals had to solve was that of ridding the body of excess salt. The kidneys can only extract a part of it. Certain species of birds, turtles, and the marine iguanas have a special gland that is used for this purpose. In the marine iguana, it is found under the eyes, but its duct empties into the nose. Occasionally, jets of water highly saturated with salt are emitted from the nose, like puffs from a vaporizer.

The dark color of the marine iguana blends in perfectly with the black lava rocks. Although this helps it to hide from predators, the dark color is mainly to regulate body heat. Since reptiles are cold-blooded, the marine iguana must face the problem of warming itself sufficiently to permit normal activity. The waters surrounding the Galápagos Islands are rather cold at about 68°F (20°C). It is known that a body cools more rapidly in water than when in contact with the air. The ideal body temperature for the iguanas is between 95° and 99°F (35° and 37°C). They cannot withstand temperature swings that lower the body temperature below 77°F (25°C) or above 104°F (40°C). When they dive into the water to feed on algae, they are subject to a rapid cooling. Therefore, the dark coloring allows them to efficiently absorb the solar radiation and thus warm themselves more quickly. The larger the animal, the longer it will take for its body to cool in the water. The adult marine

Opposite page: A peaceful land iguana warms itself in the sun while guarding its territory near a tree-cactus. Although they are smaller than the marine iguanas and the Galápagos tortoises, the land iguanas still command a certain respect. They become aggressive only when they are repeatedly disturbed. Otherwise, they always flee.

Several marine iguanas warm themselves in the sun. These lizards are even more peaceful than the land iguanas. Tameness and lack of fear of people is characteristic of almost all of the Galápagos animals. The marine iguanas must often change their positions in order to maintain their body temperature at the ideal level. They cool off rapidly in the cold ocean waters, which they must enter in order to feed on algae, their main food source. After emerging, the marine iguanas bask in the sun to heat themselves.

iguanas remain in the water longer than the young ones. The smallest iguanas feed on the beached algae without entering the water.

A black animal basking on a black rock under the tropical sun also runs the risk of overheating. A body temperature of 115°F (46°C) is deadly for the marine iguanas. To avoid overheating, the iguanas often change position, exposing only a limited portion of their bodies to the sun at one time. Otherwise, they dive into the water to cool off.

All of this points to a contradictory relationship

between the marine iguanas and the sea. The sea is the source of the marine iguana's food, but at the same time it is a stressful, dangerous environment. It is inhabited by sharks that are the marine iguana's main predators. The marine iguanas seem to be fearful of the marine environment. Even if a marine iguana is threatened on land, it normally will not dive into the water to escape. If thrown into the water, the iguana will immediately swim back to the shore. If repeatedly thrown into the water, it repeatedly comes back to land. The marine iguana is not used to facing or fleeing from predators on land since it does not have predators there.

At the beginning of the mating season, the males (especially the subspecies of the Espanola, Floreana, and Santa Fe islands) take on a brighter coloring. These brighter colors are a sign of status. The brightly colored males seek to take possession of a few square yards of territory, which they defend with challenging gestures and even fighting.

The fights between males are true tournaments with rules that are strictly respected by the two rivals. The fight is between the rightful owner of a territory and a challenger. As in every tournament, the challenger must signal its intentions to the challenged male. The challenged male, in turn, must accept the challenge.

The rivals draw close to each other side by side, walking with the legs kept stiff. The underside is raised off the ground and the crest on the back is kept erect. Both males attempt to show themselves as being larger than they actually are. They move the head up and down with a rhythm that is characteristic of the various subspecies. From the side position they move to a frontal position, and the animals rush toward one another. However, they do not bite, since, given the type of teeth that they have, biting would be dangerous for both. Instead, they push each other, head to head, like two warriors that have decided to resolve a dispute by arm wrestling.

A fight can last four or five hours until one of the fighters assumes a submissive or surrendering posture.

If a male crosses the territory of another male without the ritualized challenging display, it is attacked, bitten, and chased. This also occurs when an individual is accidently thrown into another male's territory. It appears that when the rules of chivalry are not respected, a gentlemanly challenge is transformed into a common brawl.

The mating between the male and the females that might be found in its territory follows a courtship ritual.

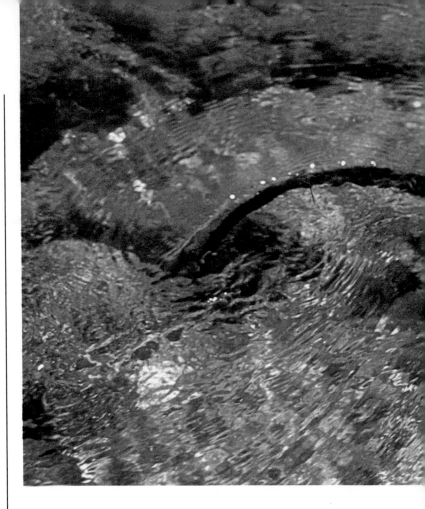

The Galápagos hawk is the only native diurnal (active during the day) bird of prey of the archipelago. What characterizes it, and at the same time threatens it, is its complete lack of fear of people. It does not fly away even if it is struck. Since the Galápagos hawks readily prey on the chickens of the islands' inhabitants, the people of the area do not hesitate to kill these birds. The preferred prey of the hawk are birds and reptiles, as well as young tortoises and iguanas.

During this ritual, the male shakes its head up and down with a type of vibration. Once the females are fertilized, they search for a suitable location to lay the eggs. Where such locations are scarce, the females will compete with each other for access. They duel in a manner similar to the males. The eggs are laid in a hole that they dig. On the island of Española, after laying the eggs, the female remains to watch the nest for several days. This is done to prevent the possible interference of other females.

The eggs hatch after about one hundred days. The newly-hatched young immediately run under a shelter and only later move toward the sea. This behavior protects them from possible predators, such as hawks, herons, and snakes. These predators prey especially on newly-hatched iguanas.

Land Iguanas

Unfortunately, even these terrifying but inoffensive lizards have recently undergone a drastic reduction in their numbers. Darwin wrote that while on the island of San Salvador (Santiago), he was unable to find a place to pitch

Marine iguanas are excellent swimmers. While swimming, they use their long, slender tails to propel themselves. They keep their legs drawn against the body.

his tent because of the numerous holes of the iguanas' dens. Today, the land iguanas are completely extinct on this island. In 1923, when the oceanographer William Beebe explored the Galápagos, land iguanas were so abundant on Baltra that one was found under every bush and cactus. Today, the iguanas are extinct on Baltra. Fortunately, several land iguanas from Baltra had been transferred to the island of Seymour. Originally, land iguanas did not inhabit Seymour Island. The introduced specimens were able to successfully reproduce.

The land iguanas belong to two species. *Conolophus subcristatus* was originally found on the islands of Fernandina, Isabela, San Salvador, Santa Cruz, Baltra, and Plaza Sud. *Conolophus pallidus* was first found on Santa Fe Island. The differences between the two species are not very clear. Some scientists consider them subspecies of the same species.

Although they are smaller than the marine iguanas, the land iguanas still are considerable in size. They can reach a length of almost 4 feet (1.2 m). The males can reach a weight

The so-called succulent plants, which have thick, juicy leaves, are adapted to arid climates. They contain important water and nutrient reserves. Many animals rely on these plants for their food and water intake. The spines serve to protect the plant from browsing animals, although they are not always effective. The photograph shows a land iguana on a blade of cactus that has fallen to the ground. The lizard is munching on a fruit with its eyes closed in order to protect them from being poked by the long spines. One often sees iguanas with cactus spines stuck around their mouths. This does not seem to seriously harm them. However, being stuck by the spines must not be very pleasant because the iguanas roll the cactus pieces on the ground to get rid of the spines before eating the fruit.

of 11 to 15 pounds (5 to 7 kg) depending on the island they inhabit. The record is 26 pounds (12 kg.) The females are considerably lighter. The color of the head, the underside, and the legs is yellow. The back is a rusty brown. The iguanas of the island of Santa Fe are the lightest in color.

The land iguanas prefer arid environments even when, as on Santa Cruz, a band of evergreen vegetation is present. They will take advantage of what is available to eat while maintaining certain preference for cacti. Land iguanas are able to remove the spines from the fruit and pieces of cactus by rolling them on the ground. During the mating season, the males establish their territories and become aggressive. In certain situations, land iguanas will blindly bite each other, but normally they avoid inflicting serious wounds.

The selection of a mating partner, however, is left to the females. Females visit various territories during a tour that can last days or even weeks. Once selected, the male remains within his territory, which can be shared with several females.

After fertilization, the females move away to search for a suitable location to lay the eggs. On the island of Fernan-

dina, the females must climb more than 3,280 feet (1,000 m) and descend approximately another 2,950 feet (900 m) to reach the preferred nesting locations in a caldera. The duration of the round-trip journey is about thirty-two days. This gives a good idea of the importance of suitable nesting locations and of their scarcity on these lava expanses. A small percentage of females lay their eggs on the slopes of the volcano.

During courtship, and also in their life as a pair, the waved albatrosses display spectacular and complicated behavior. One of the elements of a complex sequence consists of smacking the beaks, as shown in the photograph. This ritualized gesture probably comes from the process of cleaning the feathers. This type of behavior displayed by the mated pairs seems to bind their relationship. This type of activity is particularly evolved in monogamous birds. The waved albatross is a native species of the island of Española where it has a population of ten thousand. However, its hunting area extends all the way to Ecuador and Peru.

GUIDE TO AREAS OF NATURAL INTEREST

There are no particular tourist facilities in the parks associated with the pampas, the Andes mountain chain, or the Galápagos Islands. For overnight stays, it is generally necessary to leave the parks. The hotels of the Andes chain are very simple. They are similar to alpine refuges. This is also the case with the lodges in the Amazon forests. While touring the Galápagos, visitors sleep aboard ships.

There are no ideal times of the year to visit these regions. The climate is quite variable according to the latitude and the elevation. Traveling from the pampas to the Galápagos, one crosses totally different environments and seasons in the span of a little over one month. On the Colombian coast and on the Amazonian side of the Andes, the climate is warm and humid. However, it is always cool in Bogota. This city is located at an elevation of 7,870 feet (2,400 m) in the Cordillera Oriental. Along the coast of Ecuador, the climate is tropical. It is warm and humid in the forests. Quito, at an elevation of 9,185 feet (2,800 m), is characterized by a mild climate. At Guayaquil, there is airplane service to and from the Galápagos.

In Lima and along the Peruvian coast, the temperature varies between 59° and 77°F (15° and 25°C). The humidity is high, but rainfall is scarce. Lima is an oasis in the middle of a barren desert of rocks. From Lima, traveling inland by train, there are extremely different environments within a distance of 100 miles (160 km). At the end of this stretch is the park of the pampas Galeras. This park is found at an elevation of 15,092 feet (4,600 m). At Cuzco, at an elevation of 10,827 feet (3,300 m), the climate is mild and windy. Generally, on the Peruvian plateau, the rainy season lasts from November to March.

Crossing large Lake Titicaca by hydrofoil after stopping at the Island of the Sun, one reaches the Bolivian shore. In the region of La Paz, at an elevation of 13,125 feet (4,000 m), the temperature remains around 68°F (20°C) throughout the year. The climate is dry, and the nights are cool. Across the Perez Rosales pass in the Chilean park of the same name is Lake Nahuel Huapi. This is one of the most important areas of natural interest in Argentina. A dense network of roads leading to Buenos Aires cuts across the pampas. In Buenos Aires, the summer (from November to March) is warm and humid. The Rio de la Plata most certainly deserves an excursion. It is rich with bird and animal life in general. Its water is red and muddy at Buenos Aires. Toward the east, the water becomes salty.

Opposite page: One of the most striking characteristics of the animals of the Galápagos is their absolute lack of fear of people. This results from the absence of land predators on the islands. This trust suggests the image of a "paradise on earth" that humans have violated or threatened.

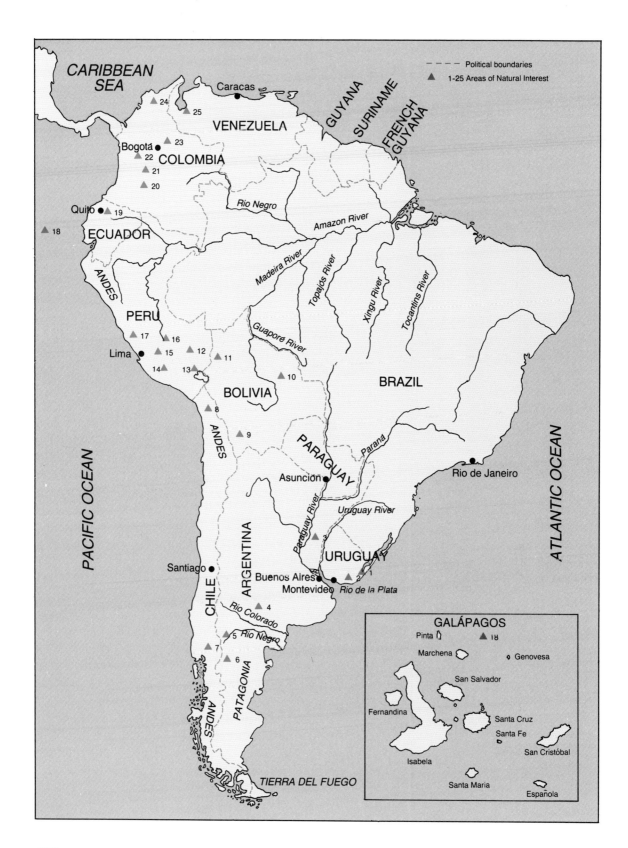

URUGUAY

Atlantic Coast (1)

The nearly 60 sq. miles (150 sq. km) of this park are located along a 16-mile (26 km) stretch of coastline with dunes as high as 197 feet (60 m). The park contains inland lagoons and marshy grasslands. They are inhabited by pampas deer and swamp deer. Both species are threatened with extinction. The swamp deer is very shy despite its large size of 220 pounds (100 kg). They spend the day hidden in the marshes and only come out at night.

This park is home to many animals that are typical of the pampas. These include the capybara, the nutria, the South American opossum, the six-banded armadillo, and the grison. The grison is a weasel-like animal with a two-colored coat. The Plata otter is only occasionally seen here. The viscacha is absent here, as it is absent in all of the Banda Oriental (Eastern band). The Uruguay River prevents it from spreading. Besides the pampas cat, the felines also include the mountain cat and the margay cat. These last two species are on the verge of extinction.

The bird populations are rich and varied. About 150 species of migratory and permanent birds inhabit the park. Aquatic and marsh birds are particularly numerous. Colonies of sea lions and fur seals live on the coast.

Banados dell'Este (2)

The vegetation of this large reserve of 772 sq. miles (2,000 sq. km), in part private, is similar to that of the humid pampas of Argentina. However, the types of plants are different. The Uruguayan pampas are characterized by "chucillas," or chains of hills that interrupt the flat line of the horizon. These pampas represent a distinct biogeographic region. However, they have many similarities with the grasslands beyond the Rio de la Plata. This reserve, along with the El Palmar park in Argentina, is one of the few parks where the ancient butia palm is protected.

Many of the native animals are still present, except for the swamp deer. The park is inhabited by a large colony of nutrias and capybaras. It is possible to see the giant otter, which is quite rare elsewhere. Several are longer than 6 feet (2 m). The streams and the lagoons of the park are ideal locations for observing migratory birds. These areas host the arriving sandpipers, albatrosses, petrels, and penguins. One of the most numerous species is the crested cariama with a black-and-white tail and a blue patch around the eyes. There are also two swan species.

The entire protected area is provided with a large network of roads. Tourist facilities are available.

Opposite page: The map indicates the main areas of natural interest of the pampas, the Andes, and the Galápagos.

Above: An extension of areas discussed are shaded: the pampas of Argentina, the Andean Cordillera, and the Galápagos Islands.

109

ARGENTINA

El Palmar (3)

This park of nearly 60 sq. miles (150 sq. km) derives its name from a forest of butia palms that is at least five hundred years old. This forest and many areas of drought-tolerant vegetation are located inside the park boundaries. Grasslands and wooded lands rich with epiphytes thrive along the rivers. This is the only park in the humid pampas of Argentina. It has many of the features of the rolling Uruguayan pampas. This region is characterized by a subtropical climate.

The viscacha and its colonies are the most visible presence in the park. Capybaras and nutrias are common along the streams. One of the endangered species in the park is the Plata otter. Jaguars can occasionally be seen in the park. In the pampas areas, there are numerous common rheas. Another large bird is the wood ibis, which is bluish black and has a hairless neck. The maguari stork, a white bird with black feathers on the shoulders and a bluish beak, also inhabits the park. The South American bittern is another inhabitant of this region. This bird makes a loud, mournful call similar to a bellow. The birds of prey include the sea eagle and the frog-eating hawk.

Lihuel Calel (4)

This park of almost 39 sq. miles (100 sq. km) is located in the southern part of the province of La Pampa. Its elevation is 1,970 to 2,300 feet (600 to 700 m). The area of the park is a good example of a dry pampa environment of scattered bushes and arid grassland. The landscape is broken up by the low Lihu Calel hills, which are of volcanic origin. The dominant plant species are shrubs that form low, spiny thickets.

Viscachas and southern cavies are common in the grasslands of the scrub zones. The jaguarundi and the pampas cat are seen only occasionally. A common small predator is the skunk. Turkey vultures and falcons are also present. The Patagonian parakeet, the crested tinamou, and the pampas flicker are widespread over the dry pampas.

This area also has a certain archaeological and historical interest. Traces of primitive civilizations can be seen in certain areas of the park. However, there are no tourist facilities, museums, or visitor centers.

Lanin (5)

The park of 750 sq. miles (1,946 sq. km) and the adjoining reserve of 710 sq. miles (1,844 sq. km) slope from an elevation of 12,140 feet (3,700 m) on the eastern side of the Andes to 1,970 feet (600 m) in an area of scrubby grassland

and dry pampa. In the band of Andean forest are Chilean pine, several species of southern beech, and Chilean cedar. Perhaps the most interesting location is the inactive volcano of Lanin, which gives the park its name. Impressive expanses of lava, hot springs, and numerous lakes of glacial origin characterize this area.

The rare southern river otter and the opossum inhabit the park. Among the most common small mammals are the nutria and the rice rat. Predatory mammals include the South American fox, the gray fox, the puma, and the South American cat. The birds of this park include two species of grebes (*Podiceps major* and *Podiceps rolland*), the Andean condor, and the southern parakeet. This bird is the southernmost parakeet, found as far south as Tierra del Fuego.

There are no tourist facilities in this park. Most of the facilities are for sport fishing since the valuable southern salmon lives in the park's waters.

Nahuel Huapi (6)

Like the preceding park, this park of 1,650 sq. miles (4,280 sq. km) also includes an Andean zone covered by forests. Rivers and lakes of glacial origin and an area of arid grassland are found within the boundaries of the park. The grassland is characterized by a Patagonian type of vegetation with drought-resistant plants. The grassland is gradually replaced by a scrub vegetation and a dry pampa. The rare pudu deer lives in the mountain environment. Although the guidebook lists the guemal as a park resident, this animal is considered extinct here. The species still survives in the park of Los Alerces in the province of Chubut. The southern river otter is occasionally seen. Precise information about its population size is not available. The opossum is quite common, and the puma and the South American cat are relatively widespread.

Aquatic birds are abundant, no doubt due to the richness of the rivers and lakes. The park is named after Lake Nahuel Huapi. Unfortunately, this lake is often crowded because the city of San Carlos de Bariloche spreads out along its shore. A colony of blue-eyed cormorants nests in the park. This is the only species of cormorant that inhabits freshwater environments. Other aquatic birds are the Magellan goose and the torrent duck. The male Magellan goose has a white head and breast. These same areas are brownish red in the female. The torrent duck is the only American duck with wing spurs.

Hotels, visitor centers, picnic areas, and campsites are

available. Most of these facilities are located in the zone of San Carlos, which is outside the park boundaries. There are also ski slopes and lifts in the area. Worth noting is the Patagonian Museum at San Carlos de Bariloque. It is dedicated to local plants and animals.

CHILE

Vincente Perez Rosales (7)

This national park of 850 sq. miles (2,200 sq. km) includes a chain of volcanic peaks. It also has a river system with its center at Lake Todos los Santos. The view from atop Cerro Pitigudo and the volcano Osorno is extraordinary. An evergreen forest represents the dominant vegetation. Clearings and marshes also abound.

The animal species are varied while not particularly abundant. There are thirty-three species of mammals in addition to over one hundred species of birds.

Lake excursions are organized at Peulla. From there, visitors depart to cross the cordillera via the Perez Rosales Pass.

Lauca (8)

This natural park of 2,007 sq. miles (5,200 sq. km) is composed of extensive plateaus at an average elevation of 14,760 feet (4,500 m). The plateau is covered by a puna type of grassland steppe, and it is crossed by rivers that flow into the Pacific Ocean.

The most common mammal is the guanaco. There are also domestic llamas, alpacas, vicunas, and guemals. One of the more notable birds is the giant coot, which builds its nest on floating mats of aquatic vegetation. Other interesting birds are the Andean gull and three species of flamingos.

BOLIVIA

Eduardo Avaroa (9)

This nature reserve of 1,545 sq. miles (4,000 sq. km), including Lake Solares, is located between the Cordillera Occidental and the Cordillera de Lipez. It is an arid zone with cacti, Azorella compacta, and saltwater lagoons filled with red water. The water is colored because of the volcanic rock. Various species of flamingos are found in the reserve. Also seen are the miner ovenbird, the Chilean avocet, and the long-billed rhea, which is widespread from Per to Patagonia. Vicunas are rare in the reserve. Predators include the puma, the South American fox, and the pampas cat. In the tall grasslands of Bolivia, this cat has a silvery gray coat with brownish red rings on the sides.

Isiboro-Secure (10)

This is a large national park that extends over an area of 4,750 sq. miles (12,300 sq. km). On the eastern side of the Andes, the land slopes from an elevation of 11,810 feet (3,600 m) to the Bolivian llanos (open, grassy plains) at an elevation of 985 feet (300 m). The vegetation varies from a cloud forest to a savanna. There are forests with many palms growing along the streams. The most visible mammals are the swamp deer and the pampas deer, as well as other deer species. There are also jaguars, pumas, Baird's tapirs and the mountain tapirs, various species of monkeys, capybaras, giant anteaters, and giant armadillos. Numerous birds, particularly the Amazon and macaw parrots, as well as many aquatic species abound.

Ulla Ulla (11)

This nature reserve of 530 sq. miles (1,380 sq. km) is found at an elevation of 14,108 feet (4,300 m). It includes one of the most extensive and tallest puna steppes, the so-called pampa de Ulla Ulla. It contains lagoons and other areas that are periodically flooded. Another reserve is located next to the Ulla Ulla reserve. The two reserves are inhabited by guemals, vicunas, and alpacas. Other inhabitants are spectacled bears, pumas, gray foxes, hog-nosed skunks, viscachas, and Bolivian field mice. There are numerous aquatic birds.

PERU

Macchu Picchu (12)

Located in the valley of the Rio Urubamba, this area of 12.5 sq. miles (32.5 sq. km) was declared a national monument. The Incan city of the same name is situated on a terrace with an elevation of 11,812 feet (3,600 m). The animals of this protected area are notable. They include the spectacled bear, the rare otter Lutra incarum, the ocelot, the pampas cat, the condor, and many snakes.

Titicaca (13)

This 140-sq. mile (361-sq. km) nature reserve encircles Lake Titicaca at an elevation of 12,468 feet (3,800 m). The relatively mild climate has temperatures varying between 48° and 57°F (9° and 14°C). The entire basin has been intensively cultivated since ancient times. Fish are abundant (salmon were introduced into the lake) as are birds. Among the birds is the crested duck, which is widespread from Peru to Tierra del Fuego. This duck has a showy crest and a brilliant red spot on the wing. There are also puna teal, teal, giant coots (coal black with a yellow-and-white spot and coral-colored legs), and flamingos.

A panoramic view of the Macchu Picchu valley in Peru is pictured. This area on the upper course of the Vilcanota River, derives its name from the ruins of an Incan village. It was rediscovered in 1911, and it is at an elevation of 11,800 feet (3,600 m).

Pampas Galeras (14)

This nature reserve of 25 sq. miles (65 sq. km) was established for the protection of the vicuna. The terrain of the reserve is a slightly rolling plateau with a pampa. It is formed of glacial and river deposits and is covered by a steppe of grasses and shrubs. Remnants of a forest of butterfly-bush and trees of the genus *Polylepis* can be observed in some areas. There are about 4,400 vicunas (this estimate was made in 1980), as well as pumas and South American foxes. The rare Andean cat with its thick coat of silvery gray hair is also found here.

Within the reserve are lodgings, a museum, vehicles, and a scientific station with a laboratory.

Huayllay (15)

This area of 26 sq. miles (68 sq. km) was declared a national monument because of the spectacular landscape features resulting from erosion. The vegetation consists of a grassland steppe with scattered trees of the genus *Polylepis*.

Mammals include the mountain viscachas, which resemble hares with their long ears and constant activity. Their tails are bushy like those of large squirrels. Other mammals present in the reserve include the gray fox and the hog-nosed skunk. This species of skunk is characterized by bristly fur with black-and-white patterns. The Andean gull is an important resident of the park. This gull is similar to the gull of the high-elevation lakes of Tibet. The rock flickers are known for their mating displays in which one partner mimes (copies) the other. The male has a red-and-black stripe above the beak. This stripe is black in the female.

Junin (16)

This nature reserve of 205 sq. miles (530 sq. km) is located in the Pampa de Junin, an extensive plain that includes Lake Junin. The reeds growing at the edge of the lake are used to make the well-known reed boats of the Andean lakes. Even the sails are made of reeds.

The lake is populated by abundant fish and amphibians. Various aquatic birds live near the shore. They include grebes and flamingos.

The administrative headquarters of the reserve in the town of Ondores can arrange lodgings for up to six people.

Huascaran (17)

This national park of 1,312 sq. miles (3,400 sq. km) is located in the Sierra Central at the same latitude as the Cordillera Blanca. Some peaks are over 19,685 feet (6,000 m) in elevation and are permanently covered with snow. El

Huascaran, the peak which gives the park its name, is at an elevation of 22,205 feet (6,768 m). It is the highest mountain in Peru. The average annual temperature is 37°F (3°C). Lows reach -22°F (-30°C). On the plateau, the woods consist primarily of trees of the genus *Polylepis* and the bromeliad *Puya raimondii*, a refuge for many species of birds.

Mammals include the northern variety of guemal, the spectacled bear, the vicuna, and the puma. Examples of birds are the torrent duck and the condor.

Lodgings are possible in a high-elevation refuge. Day trips to Punta Raymondi and the park are organized in the nearby town of Huaraz. These excursions stop at the lakes of Llanganuco at the foot of Huascaran.

ECUADOR

Galápagos (18)

The Galápagos archipelago is located 620 miles (1,000 km) off the coast of Ecuador. It is composed of thirteen major islands and many smaller islands with numerous rocks that break the surface of the water. The islands are protected as a national park and natural monument. They cover a total area of 2,668 sq. miles (6,912 sq. km).

Except for the two northernmost islands, the entire archipelago rises above a relatively shallow submarine shelf. Geologically speaking, the majority of the islands were formed in the recent past. They are composed of volcanoes and minor reliefs, the slopes of which are covered by vast expanses of lava. The water erosion in several places on the coast has caused the formation of sheer rock walls over the ocean. Sometimes, these walls give way to beaches of lava and corals. The landscape also includes lagoons formed in ancient craters, lava runoff channels, and lava fields.

Of the 650 species and subspecies of plants that grow on the islands, 36 percent are native. Stands of mangrove trees dominate the shoreline areas. Cacti of the *Opuntia*, *Brachycereus*, and *Jasminocereus thouarsii* genera dominate the arid interior. The prevalent plants in the humid zones are species of the genus *Scalesia*, guava trees, and *Pisonia fluribonda*. The high elevations are characterized by a vegetation of sedges, grasses, and ferns.

The native animals of the Galápagos are composed of invertebrates, reptiles, birds, and a few mammals. There are no amphibians. All of the reptiles, except for two species of sea turtles, are native species. Particularly noteworthy are the Galápagos tortoises (with eleven subspecies), marine iguanas, and land iguanas. The native birds include thirteen species of Galápagos finches, the flightless cormorant, the Galápagos penguin, and the Galápagos hawk. Others are the waved albatross, the lesser black-billed gull, and numerous species of Galápagos mockingbirds. The mammals are represented by rice rats, hairy-tailed bats, Galápagos fur seals, and California sea lions.

There are many signs of the disturbances caused by the introduction of animal and plant species. Numerous scientific research projects are being conducted throughout the archipelago. These group and individual projects are involved with the study of the biology and geology of the area. The Charles Darwin Scientific Station provides many facilities helpful to researchers. There are libraries, laboratories, lodgings, and means of transportation. The station is located at Puerto Ayora on the island of Santa Cruz.

Cotopaxi (19)

This national park of 131 sq. miles (340 sq. km) includes Cotopaxi, the highest active volcano in the world. Extensive high-elevation grasslands receive water from the peaks of Cotopaxi, Ruminahui, and Sincholagua. These peaks are arranged in a triangle. The park is inhabited by animals characteristic of the paramo. They include various species of deer, the cottontail rabbit, the puma, the fox, the hog-nosed skunk, the condor, falcons, doves, and the duck Anas flavirostris.

COLOMBIA

Purace (20)

This national park of 320 sq. miles (830 sq. km) is located in the Cordillera Central. It includes an active volcano with seven craters, thirty lagoons, and several waterfalls. A paramo type of vegetation is found in the high elevations. A humid forest is located at lower elevations.

The largest population of spectacled bears in Colombia is found here. Other animals are the pudu deer, a small, golden-brown deer with short velvety ears, the mountain tapir, the puma, the raccoon, and the jaguarundi. Birds include the Peruvian cock-of-the-rock, which belongs to the tyrant flycatcher family. It is widespread at the sources of the Orinoco and Amazon rivers. The male is orange-red with a crown of erect feathers on its head. Its name comes from the courtship dance performed by the male on the rocks near streams. Another noteworthy presence in the park is the quetzal, recognizable for the showy metallic green plumage of the male.

Nevado de Huila (21)

This national park of 610 sq. miles (1,580 sq. km) is located in the Cordillera Central. Its name derives from the volcano Nevado de Huila. The volcano reaches an elevation of 18,865 feet (5,750 m) and is still active. The cloud forest covering the slopes of the volcano is characterized by palms of the genus *Ceroxylon*, the national tree of Colombia. The dominant plant species of the paramo is *Espeletia hartwegiana*. Some of these individual plants reach a height of 26 feet (8 m).

Notable animals are the spectacled bear, the mountain tapir with a stout body and a black coat, the paramo deer, and various monkey species. The birds include the condor and the semicollared eagle.

Paramos de las Hermosas (22)

This natural park of 480 sq. miles (1,250 sq. km) is located in the Cordillera Central. The sources of Rioblanco, Anamichu, Amoya, Tulua, and Ambeima are all found within the park. Up to elevations between 8,200 and 9,845 feet (2,500 and 3,000 m), the land is covered by forests of podocarpus trees. The rare palm *Ceroxylon quinduense*, which is on the verge of extinction, also grows in this park. At higher elevations, there is a paramo type of vegetation.

The spectacled bear and the Brazilian tapir are well represented in this park. Both of these species are endangered. Other animals are the brocket deer and the extremely rare pacarana. This rodent is similar to the paca. It lives hidden in the forests or in cavities between rocks. The pacarana is very slow in its movements. The torrent duck is found along streams, together with the Amazon parrot *Amazona mercenaria*, a typical green parrot of the tropical zone of South America.

El Cocuy (23)

This national park of 1,181 sq. miles (3,060 sq. km) is located on the eastern side of the Cordillera Oriental. It includes glacial lakes, paramos, high terraces, and natural savannas at an elevation of 1,640 feet (500 m). The terraces are covered with a type of vegetation similar to that of the Amazon basin. Notable among the animals is the spectacled bear, which is rare and difficult to observe because of its nocturnal habits. There are margay cats and coatimundis, which are a sort of South American raccoon. Some of the birds present are condors, doves, and two tyrant flycatchers. One of the tyrant flycatchers is an antpitta (*Grallaria quitensis*) and the other is a ground tyrant (*Muscisaxicola alpina quesadae*).

Sierra Nevada de Santa Marta (24)

This national park covers an area of 1,478 sq. miles (3,830 sq. km). It includes the largest reliefs or high elevations in Colombia, such as the peak of Simon Bolivar, which is permanently covered with snow. The area has great archaeological importance.

Recently, the "Ciudad Perdida" (lost city) was discovered. This site has traces of the ancient Indian civilization of the Kogui, Arjuacos, and Tayrona tribes. The park is characterized by a series of widely different environments. These include a snowy peak, a cloud forest, and the paramo. The mammals include pumas, jaguars, giant anteaters, and Thomas' paramo mice. A large population of condors inhabits the park. Other birds include the harpy eagle, an aggressive bird with a double crest on its head. Ovenbirds, such as the shaketail ovenbird, are adapted to these high-elevation meadows. A thrush species (*Turdus fuscatercacozelus*) also lives in this area. The native species include brocket deer and small deer with small antlers. A frog species (*Geobatrachus walkari*) lives under the leaves and rocks as well as in the bases of epiphytic plants. The toad is found up to an elevation of 15,585 feet (4,750 m). Lodgings are available at the ranger center.

VENEZUELA

Sierra Nevada (25)

This national park of 1,030 sq. miles (2,670 sq. km) is located in the Sierra de Merida. It occupies a zone of reliefs covered by permanent snow, glacial lakes, paramos, cloud forest, and at lower elevations, tropical rain forest. The animals tend to be concentrated at the southern end. They include spectacled bears, pumas, jaguars, and condors.

Preceding pages: This view of the island of Daphne Major effectively illustrates a characteristic of the climate of the Galápagos. The relatively low temperature of the ocean cools the air, which makes it heavier. This prevents the upward movement of the air. When the warmer and more humid air of the upper atmospheric layers comes into contact with the cold air mass below, condensation occurs. This causes the formation of clouds and fog. However, these clouds do not produce rainfall.

GLOSSARY

adaptation change or adjustment by which a species or individual improves its condition in relationship to its environment.

archipelago a group or chain of many islands.

atmosphere the gaseous mass surrounding the earth.

biogeography the branch of biology that deals with the geographical distribution of plants and animals.

botanist a plant specialist. Botanists study the science of plants, which deals with the life, structure, growth, and classification of a plant or plant group.

carnivore a meat-eating organism such as a predatory mammal, a bird of prey, or an insectivorous plant.

conifers cone-bearing trees and shrubs, most of which are evergreens.

conservation the controlled use and systematic protection of natural resources, such as forests and waterways.

continent one of the principal land masses of the earth. Africa, Antarctica, Asia, Europe, North America, South America, and Australia are regarded as continents.

crater a bowl-shaped hole or cavity, such as the mouth of a volcano or the pit formed by a fallen meteor.

crest a tuft, ridge, or similar growth on the head of a bird or other animal.

den the cave or other home of a wild animal.

dominant that species of plant or animal which is most numerous in a community, and which has control over the other organisms in its environment.

dormant alive, but not actively growing.

ecology the relationship between organisms and their environment.

environment the circumstances or conditions of a plant or animal's surroundings.

epiphyte a plant, such as certain orchids or ferns, that grows on another plant upon which it depends for physical support but not for nutrients.

erosion natural processes such as weathering, abrasion, and corrosion, by which material is removed from the earth's surface.

evolution a gradual process in which something changes

into a different and usually more complex or better form.

extinction the process of destroying or extinguishing.

feline pertaining to a cat or the cat family.

fossil a remnant or trace of an organism of a past geologic age, such as a skeleton or leaf imprint, embedded in some part of the earth's crust.

genus a classification of plants or animals with common distinguishing characteristics.

geology the science dealing with the physical nature and history of the earth.

glaciers gigantic moving sheets of ice that covered great areas of the earth in an earlier time.

invertebrate lacking a backbone or spinal column.

lagoon a shallow body of water, especially one separated from the sea by sandbars or coral reefs.

larva the early, immature form of any animal that changes structurally when it becomes an adult.

latitude the angular distance, measured in degrees, north or south from the equator.

lava melted rock that flows from a volcano.

lichen a primitive plant formed by the association of blue-green algae with fungi.

marsh an area of low-lying flatland, such as swamp or bog.

migrate to move from one region to another with the change in seasons.

mirage an optical illusion in which the image of a distant object is made to appear nearby.

naturalist a person who studies nature, especially by direct observation of animals and plants.

niche the specific space occupied by an organism within its habitat; a small space or hollow.

nocturnal referring to animals that are active at night.

nomads people without a permanent home, who move around constantly in search of food and pasture for their animals.

oasis any fertile place in a desert, due to the presence of water.

omnivore an animal that eats both plants and other animals.

organism any individual animal or plant having diverse organs and parts that function as a whole to maintain life and its activities.

parasite an organism that grows, feeds, and is sheltered on or in a different organism while contributing nothing to the survival of its host.

peninsula a land area almost entirely surrounded by water and connected to the mainland by a narrow strip of earth called an isthmus.

plateau an elevated and more or less level expanse of land.

plumage the feathers of a bird. A bird's plumage can provide camouflage, aid in identification, and play an important role in mating rituals.

precipitation water droplets or ice particles condensed from water vapor in the atmosphere, producing rain or snow that falls to the earth's surface.

predator an animal that lives by preying on others.

prey an animal hunted or killed for food by another.

reptile a cold-blooded vertebrate having lungs, a bony skeleton, and a body covered with scales or horny plates.

salinity of or relating to the saltiness of something.

savanna a treeless plain or a grassland characterized by scattered trees, especially in tropical or subtropical regions having seasonal rains.

species a distinct kind, sort, variety, or class.

steppe a large plain having few trees.

symbiosis the living together of two kinds of organisms, especially where such an association provides benefits or advantages for both.

valley a stretch of low land lying between hills or mountains and usually having a river or stream flowing through it.

vertebrate having a backbone or spinal column.

INDEX

126

CREDITS

MAPS AND DRAWINGS. G. Vaccaro, Cologna Veneta (Verona) Italy. **PHOTOGRAPHS. Archivio 2P,** Milan: 40, 52-53, 79. **A. Borroni,** Milan: G. Mairani 26-27, 36-37, 64-65, 114-115. **M.L. Bozzi,** Turin: 13, 66, 71, 75, 98, 105. **J.M. Cei,** Lisbon: 61. **B. Lanza,** Florence: 59, 60, 104. **Marka Graphic,** Milan: 11, 32. **G. Orlando,** Palermo (Italy): 68-69, 91. **Overseas,** Milan: F. Ratti 18-19; C. Tarsitani 120-121; Jacana/F. Gohier 8, 30; NHPA/H. Palo Jr. 29; Oxford Scientific Films/G.I. Bernard 49; Oxford Scientific Films/J. Fitter 80-81, 97; Oxford Scientific Films/M.P.L. Fogden 50-51; Oxford Scientific Films/G. Merlen 76-77, 82, 86-87, 92. **Panda Photo,** Rome: S. Cedola 88; E. Coppola 42-43, 45. **D. Pellegrini,** Milan: 6-7, 16, 54, 73. **L. Pellegrini,** Milan: 14-15, 22. **F. Speranza,** Milan: A. Fatras 27, 100-101, 102-103, 106.

REFERENCE--NOT TO BE
TAKEN FROM THIS ROOM

DATE DUE

DATE DUE

574.5   Beani, Laura
Bea
         The Pampas, Andes,
         and Galapagos

                        15.00

Laramie Junior High
1355 N 22nd
Laramie, WY 82070   25602